The Style of DON JUAN

by George M. Ridenour

ARCHON BOOKS 1969

SBN: 208 00781 4
Library of Congress Catalog Card Number: 69-15690
Printed in the United States of America

For my parents

PREFACE

PERHAPS NO OTHER major poem in the language is presented with so much apology and deprecation on the part of its author as is Byron's *Don Juan;* and many readers have been inclined to take the poet at his word. When Byron does rise to defend his work, it is likely to be on purely moral grounds. But the problem for most modern readers of *Don Juan* is not the possibility of its harmful effect on the young. The difficulty seems to arise rather from the aimlessness, the apparent pointlessness of it all. Yet if *Don Juan* has any one serious defect as a work of art it is that in spite of its insistent casualness it makes its point with such single-minded perseverance. The poet's seemingly most irrelevant aside or digression is likely to turn out on examination to be another way of dramatizing his central paradox.

The underlying principle of Byron's universe seems to be that its elements are in their different ways both means of grace and occasions of sin.[1] And Byron does not let us forget it. The principle is developed primarily in terms of the traditional notions of art (especially poetry) and nature (especially as manifested in love). The implications are drama-

1. Cf. Harold Bloom, *Shelley's Mythmaking* (New Haven, Yale Univ. Press, 1959), p. 111. See also pp. 60–4. I was probably influenced in my development of this notion by Bloom.

ix

tized by means of two organizing themes, the Christian myth of the Fall and the classical rhetorical theory of the styles. The point is made again and again, as the poet investigates the possibilities of emphasis and nuance. But the poem is clearly not so static as this description would suggest: there is a third, non-thematic mode of organization, the continuing presence of the speaker or *persona*. It is this third element which, in its relations with the protagonist, makes it possible for the poem to move, to develop. The poem is, then, much more than the rehearsal of a series of paradoxes; it is a developing dramatic action (in which, of course, the paradoxes participate). I shall discuss this action in terms of development from a state of innocence to a state of experience.

But if all this structural mechanism is really in the poem, why does Byron take such pains to conceal it? The answer must be partly historical. One may think, for example, of the infinitely sophisticated Horace, and the self-conscious modesty of manner which is so much a part of his meaning. I shall therefore examine the relevance to *Don Juan* of the classical theory of the styles as transmitted especially by Cicero, Horace, Quintilian, and (most important for Byron) the English Augustans. It is the paradoxical possibilities of this theory (the senses in which the high may be low and the low high) that make it especially well adapted to express Byron's paradoxical vision.[2] The tradition, considered in terms of its metaphoric possibilities, is explored in Chapters 1 and 4. Chapters 2 and 3 are devoted to the second organizing metaphor, that of the Fall. The two are related both by their comment on the relations between the high and the low and by their involvement in the drama being enacted by the *persona*. For the speaker presents himself as

---

2. I do not think of "paradox" (or any other of the more or less technical terms I make use of) as a value word and I use these terms purely descriptively, making use of special terminology which it would be pedantic to avoid.

in the process of writing a poem which is *both* high and low.

The central importance of this stylistic tradition is one justification of the title *The Style of Don Juan*. Furthermore, I could not use a title that would seem to promise an exhaustive reading of the poem, because the monograph has no such pretensions. Nor do I propose any radical innovation in interpretation. I am trying to make sure we understand something of what we already know. In working toward this understanding, however, I shall put special emphasis on aspects of the poem (metaphor, tone, formal rhetoric) that may most conveniently be considered under the heading of style. In Chapter 5 especially I attempt some reiteration and development of the material of the earlier chapters in terms of particular ways of using language.

But I am thinking of style also in much broader terms— a "style" of life, a characteristic way of meeting and shaping experience. A striking passage from John Cowper Powys' *The Meaning of Culture* may be useful here:

> By what tenuous and filmy degrees the first outlines of a man's original philosophy precipitate themselves on the retina of his vision, like frost-marks upon a window, hardly the man himself can determine. As when a new light falls unexpectedly upon familiar things, he suddenly becomes aware of a certain pattern, a certain tone, a certain peculiar emphasis in his life's scenery which seems to satisfy at once both his good and his evil eye. What he sees seems ordered and beautiful in a particular way. He has now his own optimism, his own pessimism. The world lends itself to his interpreting imagination; lends itself to his penetrating malice.[3]

Powys is not speaking of the artist specifically, but the application is clear. So when I speak of Byron's "vision" or "world view," I am ultimately referring to what Powys, al-

3. New York, Norton, 1929, p. 11.

most as inadequately, calls "original philosophy." And though in order to express it I draw on any technique or critic or school of criticism that seems likely to be serviceable, what it is all intended to add up to is a sense of what I can only call the *style* of the poem.

This last point is my excuse for certain peculiarities of presentation. My desire to suggest what this style in its broadest sense finally means has seemed to require a degree of obliquity. Rightly or wrongly, I have made some attempt at erecting a structure (or establishing a system of relationships) that would correspond in a crude, conceptual way to Byron's imaginative construction. A practical consequence is that the chapters that make up this monograph are not designed to be read individually. Key episodes, such as the Haidée idyll, and central structural devices, such as the *persona,* are dealt with from different viewpoints in different essays. The purpose of the book, as I have implied, is not so much to make particular points as to develop a point of view.

For a study of this sort to be useful, a certain amount of polemic is probably indispensable. But it is unfortunately the case that not all of those holding the most influentially wrong-headed views of *Don Juan* have seen fit to commit themselves in print. It is my inability always to document the attitudes I am opposing that must sometimes create the impression that I am muttering indignantly to myself.

Finally, while I would like to think that people read and enjoy *Don Juan,* I would not like to think that they take it as exemplary. In a valuable essay which I saw too late to make proper use of in this study, Ernest J. Lovell, Jr., has invited us to see in *Don Juan* an example of a "poetry of action, helping man to take confidence again in himself and his society without being at all blinded to the defects or limitations of either. . . . It counsels man to live in his world and be reconciled with it, if only the more effectively to correct it." [4] This is ringing prose, and I could wish that the man who died so finely while engaged in the cause of Greek independence had written that kind of poem. There is certainly much that is noble in *Don Juan;* close acquaintance with the poem persuades one of its essential honesty. Byron is giving us the best witness he can of the vision he has gained. His vision is honest, humane, and gallant—and these are qualities permanently relevant to human life. But I cannot find it ultimately so bracing as Lovell finds it to be. What I must perceive finally in *Don Juan* is a sophistication which (in highly debased form, to be sure) we have already too much of. *Don Juan* is, I think, a beautiful, exciting, touching, and rather terrifying vision of a personal and cultural dead end. I am not sure that this is an aesthetic disadvantage. But practically it would be pernicious. I can agree with Lovell's assertion that *Don Juan* "is a poetry of clear present use" [5] only because I can believe that any work of real imaginative integrity is likely to be useful. It provides resources for the imaginative grasping and ordering of experience, and that seems to me enough utility for any poem.

I have, of course, profound obligations to many people. My greatest debt is to Frederick A. Pottle, who supervised the dissertation on *Childe Harold* from which this book developed, who read the manuscript and made valuable suggestions. Cleanth Brooks advised me as to tone. My attempts at generalization and summary are much indebted to comments made by Charles Feidelson, Jr., on an earlier stage of the work. Henri Peyre and William K. Wimsatt, Jr., provided opinions on scholarly points. Robert Burlin and

---

4. Ernest J. Lovell, Jr., "Irony and Image in Byron's *Don Juan*," in Clarence D. Thorpe, Carlos Baker, Bennett Weaver, eds., *The Major English Romantic Poets. A Symposium* (Carbondale, Ill., Southern Illinois Univ. Press, 1957), p. 148.

5. *Ibid.*

Rupert Palmer read most of the manuscript and made detailed criticism of which I have frequently taken advantage. I have obligations both general and specific to Frederick W. Hilles and Harold Bloom. David Horne edited the book efficiently and tactfully. Sir John Murray kindly sent me information regarding a manuscript in his possession and gave permission for the use of copyright material. Among critics of Byron I have found the works of Elizabeth French Boyd, Sir Herbert Grierson, and Ernest J. Lovell, Jr., most congenial.

G. M. R.

New Haven, Conn.
September 1959

SHORT TITLES

LJ   Rowland E. Prothero, ed., *The Works of Lord Byron, Letters and Journals,* 6 vols. London, John Murray, 1898–1901.

Poetry   Ernest Hartley Coleridge, ed., *The Works of Lord Byron, Poetry,* 7 vols. London, John Murray, 1898–1905.

Variorum Truman Guy Steffan and Willis W. Pratt, eds., *Don Juan,* 4 vols. (Vol. 1, T. G. Steffan, *The Making of a Masterpiece;* Vols. 2 and 3, T. G. Steffan and W. W. Pratt, eds., *A Variorum Edition;* Vol. 4, W. W. Pratt, *Notes on the Variorum Edition*), Austin, Univ. of Texas Press, 1957.

CONTENTS

Chapter 1

"HONEST SIMPLE VERSE"

BYRON'S DEDICATION to *Don Juan* is a brilliant, self-contained satire in the Augustan manner. It is also highly relevant to the poem it was designed to precede. On both counts it deserves careful attention.

The Dedication begins with an extended attack on the Laureate—"Bob Southey!" And while it is no secret that Byron heartily disliked Southey personally (while paying tribute to his prose and heroic figure), the older poet is being presented primarily as a type. It is his representative aspect (increased by his being Laureate) that is to be emphasized. He embodies a disease that has become epidemic of late, especially among poets ("a common case"), and it is the satirist's function to diagnose the "case" and expose the real nature of the infection. For even if chances of saving the victim himself seem slight, society may yet be protected from a further spread of the disease:

> Bob Southey! You're a poet—Poet-laureate,
>   And representative of all the race;
> Although 'tis true that you turned out a Tory at
>   Last,—yours has lately been a common case;
> And now, my Epic Renegade! what are ye at?
>   With all the Lakers, in and out of place?

1

A nest of tuneful persons, to my eye
Like "four and twenty Blackbirds in a pye;

"Which pye being opened they began to sing,"
　(This old song and new simile holds good),
"A dainty dish to set before the King,"
　Or Regent, who admires such kind of food;—
And Coleridge, too, has lately taken wing,
　But like a hawk encumbered with his hood,—
Explaining Metaphysics to the nation—
I wish he would explain his Explanation.[1]　　[1–2]

Southey is, we are told, an "Epic Renegade." The epithet suggests the two areas of value with which the satire is principally concerned, the literary and the social (or political). Like Pope and the Augustans, Byron is assuming that the two are not unrelated. "Epic," of course, refers to the long, heavy, and above all pretentious "epics" that "Bob Southey" produced "every spring" (III.97), while "Renegade" is a by no means oblique allusion to Southey's political inconstancy. There is, it is suggested, a connection between bad poetry and bad politics. The basis is the traditional belief that a bad man cannot be a good poet. This is a fundamental presupposition of Augustan satire, notably *The Dunciad.* And there is the further suggestion that Southey is also a traitor against the truly epic.

In the last line of the first stanza Byron introduces the bird image, which he will shortly generalize into the centrally important image of flight. The use of the Mother Goose rhyme of the "four and twenty Blackbirds" is a fine example of what in an Augustan satire we should be invited to admire as a "diminishing figure." The song of the blackbirds diminishes or makes ridiculous the poetry of Southey

---

1. All quotations from Byron's verse are taken from the edition of E. H. Coleridge, *The Works of Lord Byron, Poetry,* 7 vols. London, John Murray, 1898–1904 (cited as *Poetry*).

and his friends the "Lakers," while the fact that in the nursery rhyme the blackbirds are "baked in a pie" and "set before the King" enables the satirist further to ridicule what Byron and many others considered the poets' prostitution of their talents in the service of tyranny. So both social and literary elements are again combined, this time in a popular nursery rhyme, which fact is itself an effective instrument of diminution.

In the fifth line of the second stanza Byron modulates to an image of flight. The satirist singles out one of the "blackbirds," who is now seen as a hawk who has "taken wing" before his hood has been removed. The political element is recessive for the moment (though Coleridge too was a renegade from Byron's point of view), and the satire is in the tradition of Swift and the Scriblerus Papers. Coleridge is being considered primarily as a metaphysician. Now Byron had a thoroughly Augustan contempt for metaphysics. It is, from his point of view, an absurdly pretentious theorizing on matters either inaccessible to the human intellect or irrelevant to human life. The hawk is soaring off into the skies, but, hooded, it can see even less than the spectator on the ground.

> You, Bob! are rather insolent, you know,
>   At being disappointed in your wish
> To supersede all warblers here below,
>   And be the only Blackbird in the dish;
> And then you overstrain yourself, or so,
>   And tumble downward like the flying fish
> Gasping on deck, because you soar too high, Bob,
> And fall, for lack of moisture, quite a-dry, Bob!   [3]

Byron returns to Southey in the third stanza, remarking on the arrogance of wanting to be "the only Blackbird in the dish," and picking up again the notion of the soaring flight, here applied specifically to poetry. The terms are still

Scriblerian. The Laureate, in his "insolent" striving for a supremacy not his by nature, "overstrains" himself. And ever since Icarus the result of trying to fly higher than one is able has been to suffer a fall. For as Bullitt has pointed out with regard to the satire of Swift, height and depth meet.[2] What Bullitt says of Swift is equally true of Byron:

> As a technique of satire this perception of the bordering frontiers of height and depth provided Swift with a ready visual framework in which abstract ideas or emotional reactions could be fleshed with concrete imagery. . . . To the visual idea of height Swift added the concrete connotations of many things which, through common association, are thought to rise; thus, air rises, and fire and scum and oil. Similarly, the connotations of depth are associated with heavy things which sink or fall, with excessive materiality, with dullness, stupidity, and thickheadedness.[3]

Here the Laureate, in suffering his fall, is further diminished to a flying fish gasping for air on the deck of a ship (he is "out of his element").

2. John M. Bullitt, *Jonathan Swift and the Anatomy of Satire* (Cambridge, Harvard Univ. Press, 1953), esp. pp. 181–92. (I shall refer throughout this chapter to Bullitt's book, which serves as a handy reference volume of Scriblerian technique.) Byron uses the imagery frequently in his other satires. Note especially:

> From soaring Southey, down to groveling Stott.
> [*English Bards*, l. 142]

> One falls while following Elegance too fast;
> Another soars, inflated with Bombast.
> [*Hints from Horace*, ll. 43–4]

> Beware—for God's sake, don't begin like Bowles!
> "Awake a louder and a loftier strain,"—
> And pray, what follows from his boiling brain?—
> He sinks to Southey's level in a trice. [Ibid., ll. 194–7]

3. Bullitt, p. 183.

And Wordsworth, in a rather long "Excursion,"
    (I think the quarto holds five hundred pages),
Has given a sample from the vasty version
    Of his new system to perplex the sages;
'Tis poetry—at least by his assertion,
    And may appear so when the dog-star rages—
And he who understands it would be able
To add a story to the Tower of Babel.

You—Gentlemen! by dint of long seclusion
    From better company, have kept your own
At Keswick, and, through still continued fusion
    Of one another's minds, at last have grown
To deem as a most logical conclusion,
    That Poesy has wreaths for you alone:
There is a narrowness in such a notion,
Which makes me wish you'd change your lakes
        for Ocean.   [4–5]

Poetic and philosophic elements are combined again in the stanza (4) on Wordsworth, who is guilty first of all of having produced a "new system." Like the Scriblerians, Byron had a strong distrust of all system ("When a man talks of his system, it is like a woman's talking of her *virtue*. I let them talk on").[4] The word suggested pretension, obscurity, and irrelevance to actual living. There was something overweening about the very attempt at constructing a system, a notion nicely suggested by the casual reference to the Tower of Babel. Here again the notion of pride, height, and fall (the story of the destruction of the tower is, of course, nonbiblical, but the idea is a natural and a common one). And the "linguistic" aspect of the story gives it special point.

4. From Byron's second letter on the Bowles Controversy, *The Works of Lord Byron, Letters and Journals*, ed. Rowland E. Prothero (6 vols. London, John Murray, 1898–1901), 5, 588. This will be cited as *LJ*.

Stanzas five through seven are addressed to the Lakers as a group. They are accused first of all of provinciality. They are intellectually inbred, cut off from the main currents of life,[5] and the fact that they happen to be associated in the public mind with the lakes of Cumberland makes possible a neat comment on the relative narrowness of range suggested by a lake as compared with an ocean. Also, they are accused of venality. The sixth stanza overflows with such words as "coin," "gold," "price," "salary," "place." They are men for hire (cf. Richard Savage's *An Author to Be Let*).

> For me, who, wandering with pedestrian Muses,
>   Contend not with you on the wingéd steed,
> I wish your fate may yield ye, when she chooses,
>   The fame you envy, and the skill you need.
> And, recollect, a poet nothing loses
>   In giving to his brethren their full meed
> Of merit—and complaint of present days
> Is not the certain path to future praise.[6]   [8]

5. It may be worth mentioning that this point is emphasized by Byron's friend Francis Hodgson in the prefatory note to his translation of Juvenal's Third Satire (*The Satires of Juvenal*, London, 1807, p. 32): "How much more free from that peculiarity of manner, which has debased their best performances, would the enthusiasts of a certain literary lake have shown themselves, had they mingled more largely in the world; had they caught and compared the various lights and shades of character, and submitted their singular tenets, with regard to poetical energy and simplicity, to the tribunal of learned and liberal discussion."

6. Willis W. Pratt suggests, very plausibly, that Byron's references to the poet's reliance on "future praise" may be an allusion to the lines from the "Epilogue to the Lay of the Laureate" which he quotes in the last stanza of Canto I (*Byron's Don Juan*, ed. Truman Guy Steffan and Willis W. Pratt [4 vols. Austin, Univ. of Texas Press, 1957], *4*, 11. To be cited as *Variorum*). It is more likely, however, that Byron is thinking primarily of Wordsworth's comments on the subject in the "Essay, Supplementary to the Preface" (to *Lyrical Ballads*), where the disparagement of contemporary popularity was hardly calculated to conciliate the most spectacularly popular poet of the age. See *Don Juan*, IV.109, and E. H. Coleridge's note (*Poetry*, 6, 214).

At this point a new element is introduced into the image of flight, one related to but by no means identical with the range of meanings already presented. In the opposition between the "wingéd steed" and the "pedestrian Muses" we have to deal with the traditional and vexing problem of the theory of styles, a part of the general concept of literary decorum. Certain attitudes, topics, and circumstances demand certain modes of expression. Social, moral, and literary hierarchies are elaborately related to each other.[7]

It would have been next to impossible to have read the Augustans as industriously and piously as Byron did without having absorbed a good deal of their thought on the subject of style. An eighteenth-century poet publishing a work of any magnitude was very likely to supply a preface explaining and justifying his use of a particular verse form and of particular kinds of language. (Byron is following in this tradition in the last paragraph of his preface to the first two cantos of *Childe Harold.*) I quote the rather full characterization provided by Pope in one of his notes to the *Iliad* (Bk. iii, l. 135), a work Byron had known since childhood. Commenting on a speech of Menelaus, Pope suggests the differences between the traditional stylistic modes in terms of the characteristic oratorical manner of Nestor, Ulysses, and Menelaus himself (I omit the speech of Nestor, which embodies the intermediate or "middle" style):

> Had it been Ulysses who was to make the speech, he would have mentioned a few of their affecting calamities in a pathetick air; then have undertaken the fight with testifying such a chearful joy, as should have won

7. The best discussion of the classical tradition I know is George Converse Fiske's *Lucilius and Horace. A Study in the Classical Theory of Imitation*, University of Wisconsin Studies in Language and Literature, 7, Madison, 1920. A good deal of material on the eighteenth century's understanding of the tradition is to be found in Ian Jack's *Augustan Satire. Intention and Idiom in English Poetry, 1660–1750*, Oxford, Clarendon Press, 1952.

the hearts of the soldiers to follow him to the field without being desired. He would have been . . . solemn, rather than particular, in speaking of the rites, which he would only insist on as an opportunity to exhort both sides to a fear of the Gods, and a strict regard of justice. . . . For a conclusion, he would have used some noble sentiment agreeable to a hero, and (it may be) have enforced it with some inspirited action. In all this you would have known that the discourse hung together, but its fire would not always suffer it to be seen in cooler transitions, which (when they are too nicely laid open) may conduct the reader, but never carry him away. The people would hear him with emotion.

These materials being given to Menelaus, he but just mentions their troubles, and his satisfaction in the prospect of ending them, shortens the proposals, says a sacrifice is necessary, requires Priam's presence to confirm the conditions, refuses his sons with a resentment of that injury he suffered by them, and concludes with a reason for his choice from the praise of his age, with a short gravity, and the air of an apothegm. This he puts in order without any more transition than what a single conjunction affords. And the effect of the discourse is, that the people are instructed by it in what is to be done.[8]

The passage is of particular value because it does not raise the confusing and largely irrelevant questions of social and topical decorum. The speakers are princes and they are speaking on the same subject. It is their attitude toward and mode of dealing with the material (and the effect it is calculated to have on its audience) which forms the basis of stylistic discrimination. According to Cicero (*Orator* xxi.69)

8. Gilbert Wakefield, ed. (6 vols. London, 1796), 2, 20–1.

and Quintilian (*Institutio Oratoria* XII.x.59) the function of the three styles is to instruct (the "plain"), to "charm" (the "middle"), and move (the "high," or "grand"). The distinction is made with reference to intention (or function) and relative intensity. In terms of the rhetorical tradition, then, Ulysses' speech would be an example of the high style of impassioned utterance, Menelaus' of the plain style of factual discourse.

But while the characterization of the high style is clear enough, Pope's anxiety to make a clear distinction between *three* styles has led him to distort slightly the description of the plain. In his comments on Menelaus' speech he has omitted any mention of the "delight" (*iucunditas*) ascribed to this same speech in the passage of Quintilian (*Inst. Orat.* XII.x.64–5) which is the unacknowledged (and, I gather, unnoticed) basis of his gloss. The plain style is, to be sure, that of the so-called *musa pedestris* (Byron's "pedestrian Muses") of Horace (*Serm.* II.VI.17). The most important fact about it is that, as Pope observes (following Cicero and Quintilian), it "instructs"—it tells the truth. It is significant that Pope himself has translated Horace's characterization of his own satires (in the *musa pedestris* passage mentioned above) as "Something in Verse as *true* as Prose" ("The Sixth Satire of the Second Book of *Horace*," l. 26; my italics). But obviously neither Horace nor Pope is so dry as the description of Menelaus would suggest. While "charm" is rather arbitrarily assigned to the curious and ill-defined "middle style," the plain is not without its own delights.[9] It is, in fact, the social mode *par excellence*. Cicero describes it as the mode of wit and good-natured raillery (*Orator* XXVI.87 ff.). It is a mode of amiability and conciliation, in contrast with the savage invective of the diatribe. It is a mode of elegant sim-

---

9. In the remainder of this paragraph I am heavily indebted to Mary A. Grant, *The Ancient Rhetorical Theories of the Laughable*, University of Wisconsin Studies in Language and Literature, 21, Madison, 1924.

plicity. It is, in short, the urbane and highly civilized mode of Horace and the *De Officiis*. Mary Grant describes the humor proper to the plain style:

> As the *sermo*, written in the plain style, was informal, relaxed, and kindly in tone, so laughter, which is suited to banquets and times of recreation was suitably associated with it. Among the different kinds of humor, the mild and pervasive type of Socratic irony, subtle in its half-laughter and half-earnestness, harmonized best with the ease and affability of the *sermo*, its change of tone from grave to gay, its art in the absence of art.[1]

Byron is clearly thinking in terms of this tradition when he begins the eighth stanza with a contrast between himself and the Lakers. While they ride (or try to ride) "the wingéd steed" of heroic poetry, he contents himself with "wandering with pedestrian Muses." They strive for the high style of the heroic and sublime, he for the plain style of gentlemanly discourse. By implication he is also continuing his comment on the provinciality of the Lakers, paradoxically associating the solitary flight of the poet on his Pegasus (with all the enormous prestige traditionally involved in the idea of heroic verse) with selfishness, egotism, and other antisocial qualities that are in contrast to the highly social implications of the "pedestrian Muses" he has elected to serve. There is something of this notion present in the sometimes curiously sardonic comments Byron makes on the epic mode in the course of his own epic satire.[2]

If, fallen in evil days on evil tongues,
    Milton appealed to the Avenger, Time,

1. Grant, p. 138.

2. Horace had earlier insisted on a contrast between his "chats" and the high style of epic, but he had not ventured to challenge the authority of the epic mode itself. See Lucius Rogers Shero, "The Satirist's *Apologia*," University of Wisconsin Studies in Language and Literature, 15; Classical Studies, Series, 2 (Madison, 1922), pp. 148–67, esp. 155 and n. 5, 163 n. 21.

If Time, the Avenger, execrates his wrongs,
    And makes the word "Miltonic" mean *"Sublime,"*
He deigned not to belie his soul in songs,
    Nor turn his very talent to a crime;
He did not loathe the Sire to laud the Son,
But closed the tyrant-hater he begun.

Think'st thou, could he—the blind Old Man—arise
    Like Samuel from the grave, to freeze once more
The blood of monarchs with his prophecies,
    Or be alive again—again all hoar
With time and trials, and those helpless eyes,
    And heartless daughters—worn—and pale—and poor;
Would *he* adore a sultan? *he* obey
The intellectual eunuch Castlereagh?   [10–11]

In the tenth stanza stylistic allusions are subjected to
further complication in terms of social values. Characteristically, Byron develops his values in terms of an individual
personality, in this case Milton. Milton, we are told, fell "in
evil days on evil tongues." He *fell* because he would not *rise*
by betraying his convictions. He would not, that is, act as
Southey and his friends have acted. And as the result of this
fall a fine Byronic Nemesis (Time, the Avenger) has pro-
claimed Milton's true poetic *height* (etymological pun on
"Sublime"). A correlation, therefore, is suggested between
moral and political integrity and poetic achievement corre-
sponding to that noted earlier, with regard to Southey.

In these stanzas the tone of the poem undergoes a dramatic shift. Thus far it has been that of discourse, conversation—the plain style and the pedestrian muses. Now, in a
kind of prosopopœia (a device especially characteristic of
the high style), he has a vision of Milton rising from his
grave like Samuel and surveying the present state of things.
Milton is seen as a prophet in the Hebraic tradition (commonly acknowledged as a particularly potent form of the

sublime). And Byron's own manner takes on something of the prophetic. Or, more precisely, perhaps, he rises from the urbane raillery of Horace to the heroic invective of Juvenal.

And again the argument is developed in terms of a specific personality—Castlereagh. There is, according to the satirist, something sterile about Castlereagh. He is an "intellectual eunuch." He is emasculated, a Eutropius, an It; for tyranny, which Castlereagh embodies, is seen as essentially sterile. But it is sinister and it is dangerous (the technique of associating the subject to be ridiculed with sexual impotence is, of course, a traditional one; but the connection between impotence and lust for power exists on a much deeper level than that of mere invective).[3] As with Southey, it is not simply a matter of personal animus on Byron's part (he had no contact with Castlereagh personally). It is as a social force that Castlereagh is so unequivocally denounced. And the denunciation follows a pattern which should be thoroughly familiar to us by now. In the twelfth stanza it is the political, in the thirteenth the literary, aspect that is stressed —and both are permeated with a feeling of impotence and incapacity. Castlereagh is not only a

> Cold-blooded, smooth-faced, placid miscreant!
>   Dabbling its sleek young hands in Erin's gore,

but also

3. Cf. Bullitt, pp. 46–7. Byron's most recent biographer has called attention to what turns out to be a highly relevant obscenity in the last line of Dedication 3: Leslie A. Marchand, *Bryon. A Biography* (3 vols. New York, Knopf), 2, 763 n. Byron makes good use of the theme again in his savage lines on Milman (XI.58). While "neutralized" and "Sporus" have always been clear enough, it seems only recently to have been pointed out (by Aurélien Digeon, in the notes to his edition of the poem for the Collection Bilingue des Classiques Etrangers, 2 vols. Paris, Aubier, n.d., 2, 610) that Dorus is a eunuch slave in Terence's *Eunuchus*. The priests of Cybele were, of course, also eunuchs.

An orator of such set trash of phrase
    Ineffably—legitimately vile,
That even its grossest flatterers dare not praise.

                                              [12, 13]

Byron returns to this theme in the preface to Cantos VI, VII, and VIII, where he observes: "It is the first time indeed since the Normans that England has been insulted by a *minister* (at least) who could not speak English, and that Parliament permitted itself to be dictated to in the language of Mrs. Malaprop." [4] The invective reaches its peak of intensity in the fourteenth stanza:

A bungler even in its disgusting trade,
    And botching, patching, leaving still behind
Something of which its masters are afraid—
    States to be curbed, and thoughts to be confined,
Conspiracy or Congress to be made—
    Cobbling at manacles for all mankind—
A tinkering slave-maker, who mends old chains,
With God and Man's abhorrence for its gains.   [14]

While earlier Castlereagh has been described as a "tool" of tyrants whose oratory is an "Ixion grindstone's ceaseless toil" (13), he is now a workman, a chain-maker (or mender), and not even a good one. Apart from the general "tinker" image, the stanza makes its satiric point through a skillful use of verbal and aural patterns. The two strongest words of the first line, "bungler" and "disgusting," support each other by means of their common *uh* sound. "Botching" and "patching" of the second line pick up the *-ing* of "disgusting" and are reinforced by their common *tch* sound. "Leaving" and "Something" carry on the *-ing* rhyme. Line four is balanced syntactically and aurally (the alliteration of "curbed" and "confined"). The fifth line presents a fine

4. *Poetry, 6,* 285. Cf. *Don Juan,* IX.49.

Augustan juxtaposition ("Conspiracy or Congress"),[5] again reinforced by alliteration and assonance (echoing line four). "Cobbling" in line six continues the succession of alliterating voiceless gutturals and is followed by the play on *"mana*cles" and *"man*kind" (the tyrant thinks of man as something to be manacled). The devices are obvious enough, but they are used here to fine effect, supporting the passionate contempt of the tinker image.

What has happened? Byron's basic structural device is again a traditional one, used to greatest brilliance, perhaps, in the two dialogues of Pope's "Epilogue to the Satires." Like Pope, Byron carefully reminds us of the traditional distinction between the high style of passion and the plain style of polite discourse (the "correctness" of the third line of the First Dialogue),[6] announces his own allegiance to the second, and then allows his righteous indignation to carry him to that same heroic level he had previously modestly renounced. *He,* then, is truly soaring on Pegasus. But *his* eyes are not blinded like the hawk's, and, if he does not always choose to write in the more ambitious mode, it is not because he (like Southey, who does so choose, and fails) cannot do so if he will. His aim, like any satirist's, is truth. Truth normally demands a quiet tone, a plain manner, like the speech of Menelaus.[7] But truth is something to which

5. Cf. Bullitt (p. 45): "A similarity may be drawn between an object and one which is universally acknowledged to be inferior; the comparison results, of course, in the primary object absorbing the contemptibility of the secondary object."

6. "You grow *correct,* that once with *Rapture* writ" (my italics). Cf. Fiske (p. 127) on the *Latinitas,* which is a primary characteristic of the plain style. It is "correctness and purity of conversational idiom employed in accordance with the tenets of technical grammatical theory . . . in the language of colloquial art, but not of the streets." This is as good a definition of Popean "correctness" as one could wish. "Rapture" refers to the passion or sublimity of the high style. Pope so uses the word in the preface to his *Iliad* (ed. Wakefield, *1,* xxviii).

7. For the connection between truth and the plain style see Fiske, p. 78.

one is committed. It is a value which justifies the most rapturous of tones in its defense and which has in itself the power to elevate the lowest discourse. As Byron had written years before in *English Bards* (referring specifically to Crabbe):

> There be who say, in these enlightened days,
> That splendid lies are all the poet's praise;
> That strained Invention, ever on the wing,
> Alone impels the modern Bard to sing:
> 'Tis true, that all who rhyme—nay, all who write,
> Shrink from that fatal word to Genius—Trite;
> *Yet Truth sometimes will lend her noblest fires,*
> *And decorate the verse herself inspires.*[8]

[ll. 849–56]

Byron, in the vindication of the truth as he sees it, rises to the heroic mode, thus asserting himself as a satirist in the grand tradition of his master Pope (and Horace and Juvenal). In doing so, he is dramatizing one of the senses in which his poem is "epic." [9]

The tone descends rapidly at the end of stanza sixteen, as the satirist unites himself with the voices of the oppressed peoples of Europe, while identifying Southey with the op-

---

This supplies the structural basis of the Second Dialogue of the "Epilogue to the Satires." Cf. ll. 246–7:

> Truth guards the Poet, sanctifies the line,
> And makes Immortal, Verse as mean as mine.

"Mean" here is used technically, with reference to the low style. Cf. the Juvenalian *Facit indignatio versum (Sat. 1.79).*

8. The passage I have put in italics is patently modeled on the lines of Pope quoted in the preceding note. For the connection between anger and the high style see Grant, p. 134. See also Horace, *Serm.* I.X.11–13 (used by Pope as epigraph to the *Moral Essays*) and *Ars Poetica,* ll. 93–4.

9. What is important, of course, is not that Bryon's tone has grown more intense in the course of his poem—that is not remarkable—but that we have been given a structure in terms of which this tonal heightening, occurring when it does and the way it does, takes on metaphoric significance.

pressors ("And Southey lives to sing them very ill"). The final note is that of the "honest simple verse" of the *musa pedestris:*

> Meantime, Sir Laureate, I proceed to dedicate,
>   In honest simple verse, this song to you.
> And, if in flattering strains I do not predicate,
>   'Tis that I still retain my "buff and blue;"
> My politics as yet are all to educate:
>   Apostasy's so fashionable, too,
> To keep *one* creed's a task grown quite Herculean;
> Is it not so, my Tory, ultra-Julian?   [17]

The verse is honest because it has not been "sold," prostituted. It is simple in that it is not pretentiously, obscurely "soaring." The last stanza, in short, summarizes in a mode of urbane mockery the central issues of the Dedication.

Byron has chosen, then, to introduce his longest and most ambitious work with an elaborately traditional satire in the Augustan manner. And the prologue reflects on the satirical epic itself in any number of ways. Consider, for example, the question of the *persona,* that traditional formal device of supplying oneself with an organized personality to function as speaker. Critics overcome by the poet's own well-publicized personality have evidently considered the notion of a *persona* quite irrelevant to Byron. But simply from a formalistic standpoint, one should perhaps recall that satire is a kind that traditionally invites the exploitation of personality on the part of the author. If there is a great deal of Byron in *Don Juan,* there is a very great deal of Horace and Juvenal and Pope in their satires. All four poets enter their works, attack personal enemies, and air personal prejudices. And all four generalize the personal to a level relevant to society as a whole. In the Dedication Byron is speaking from behind the traditional satiric mask. He is a modest man (content with pedestrian muses) who writes "honest simple verse"—in other words, the plain blunt man we have been taught to recognize in Augustan satire. He is a man with both feet on the ground who prefers to chat quietly as one gentleman to another, but who is prepared to raise his voice when truth as he sees it or civilized standards as he has received them seem threatened. We learn from the poem itself that he is not a man without faults, but what faults he has are at least those of passion and indiscretion, not of calculation, venality, self-conceit, or an impotence which manifests itself in tyranny (to restrict ourselves for the moment to the vices dealt with in the Dedication). The nature and function of the *persona* will develop greatly in the course of the poem. But the *persona* remains central, and the significance of the speaker of the cantos is largely dependent on values first brought out in terms of the more conventional speaker of the Dedication.

Furthermore, we have most certainly not heard the last of that connection between the literary and the social on which the Dedication so insists. The motif will not only be present in Byron's recurrent attacks on other writers (especially the Lakers), but will also undergo elaborate development in terms of the concept of epic. For we are to be persistently reminded that "My poem is epic," and the implications of that statement are at least as much moral as literary. Further, insofar as *Don Juan* is a satire of European society, there are obvious advantages in introducing the figure of the traditional satiric *persona,* the *civis* par excellence. The pose adopted in the Dedication should serve to prepare us for a certain seriousness of purpose in the body of the poem. It should also make us sensitive to the use of pose in the speaker himself. One aspect of this pose, the speaker's insistence on his own knowledge of the world, is obviously closely related to the opposition between provinciality and cosmopolitanism first developed in the Dedication. And not only the speaker, but also the protagonist, is to be a world

traveler and cosmopolite. Furthermore, the one thing every
reader would know about the protagonist, Don Juan, is that
he is a kind of archetypal great lover. When one thinks,
then, of the use of the images of sterility and impotence in
the Dedication, one is prepared to find the impotence of
tyrants opposed by a hero who is a successful lover, with no
compulsion to compensate for his own inadequacy by bully-
ing other people. And, finally, there is the whole complex of
stylistic concepts that, beginning with the Dedication, will
grow throughout the whole poem, serving as one of its
organizing metaphors. The traditional associations of epic
and satire are constantly being played against each other in
the course of defining the sense in which a satire may be
epic.

Chapter 2

"A WASTE AND ICY CLIME"

ONE OF THE PRINCIPAL obstacles to an appreciation of *Don Juan* on the part of many serious readers of poetry in our day has been what seems to them the irresponsible nature of Byron's satire. They feel that, clever as the poem undoubtedly is in parts, taken as a whole it is immature, exhibitionistic, lacking in integrity. This has caused distress on both moral and aesthetic grounds. But though it is not prudery to refuse assent to the implications of the poet's vision, it would be unjust to deny due praise to the style of that vision—its special grace and swagger. Certain obvious faults in the manner of the poem may be frankly conceded. Byron is sometimes careless, and there are times when he is obviously showing off. Sometimes, though rarely in *Don Juan,* he is guilty of bad taste.

But it is not these things, I suspect, that constitute the real problem. It has more to do with the uncertainty of the satirist's point of view as compared, say, with Horace or Pope. Satirists are normally conservatives and are proceeding at least ostensibly on the basis of a generally accepted (or in any case familiar) system of norms, principles, and attitudes. That this is not true of Byron in the way in which it is true of Horace or Pope (though the consistency of both

19

is liable to some criticism) is clear enough. Byron is notoriously a rebel, and rebels have not enjoyed high critical esteem lately.

But Byron is not a consistent rebel. There is, for example, his apparently snobbish insistence on Juan's birth and breeding. And his views on women would hardly commend themselves to emancipated spirits. But then what were Byron's views on women (or aristocrats)? They seem to undergo such remarkable shifts in the course of sixteen cantos that it is not easy to say. The apparent lack of structure in terms of which these shifting points of view can be assimilated is, I gather, the basic problem of *Don Juan* for the modern reader.[1] It is not so much "What does he stand for?" (that is not always self-evident in the most traditional of satires), as "How do his various professions fit together?" In short, is *Don Juan* a chaos or a unity?

The question is natural and not unanswerable. The answer, however, cannot be in terms of a system. I have already pointed out that, even more than his Scriblerian predecessors, Byron had a temperamental aversion to system. He is not to be categorized either intellectually or poetically. But this is not to say that his vision is incoherent. It is, in fact, elaborately coherent. And it is with what seem to me the dominant modes of this coherence that I shall be largely concerned.

In the first place, Byron, rebel that he is, is perfectly willing to make use of traditional concepts for his own ends. Some elements of the Christian myth especially commended themselves to him both as man and as poet. Whether it was the result of the Calvinistic influences of Byron's Scottish childhood, whether it was temperamental, aesthetic, the product of his own experience, or any combination of these

1. This difficulty is not exclusively modern. One of the best statements is to be found in Hazlitt's essay on *Vathek*.

factors, Byron seems throughout his life to have had peculiar sympathy with the concept of natural depravity. Lovell has asserted that "Byron held consistently to a belief in the existence of sin and the humanistic ideal of virtue as self-discipline. The fall of man—however he resented the injustice of its consequences—is the all-shadowing fact for him." [2] Whatever one may think of this as a biographical generalization, it is clearly true of the imagination of the poet of *Don Juan*—with the reservation that in the poem the Christian doctrine of the Fall is a *metaphor* which Byron uses to express his own personal vision. In *Childe Harold*, as we shall see, he developed an original reading of the Prometheus myth for similar purposes.

The myth of the Fall, then, is an important means of organizing the apparently contradictory elements of *Don Juan*. In the context of Byron's reading of the myth, Helene Richter's and William J. Calvert's interpretation of Byron in terms of a classic-romantic paradox and Antonio Porta's very similar Rousseau-Voltaire split are seen as elements in a vision not readily to be categorized under any of these headings.[3]

Byron introduces Canto IV with a stanza on the perils of poetry:

> Nothing so difficult as a beginning
>   In poesy, unless perhaps the end;
> For oftentimes when Pegasus seems winning
>   The race, he sprains a wing, and down we tend,
> Like Lucifer when hurled from Heaven for sinning;

2. Ernest J. Lovell, Jr., *Byron: The Record of a Quest. Studies in a Poet's Concept and Treatment of Nature* (Austin, Univ. of Texas Press, 1949), p. 250.

3. Helene Richter, *Lord Byron. Persönlichkeit und Werk* (Halle, Niemeyer, 1929), pp. 126–43. William J. Calvert, *Byron. Romantic Paradox* (Chapel Hill, Univ. of North Carolina Press, 1935), passim. Antonio Porta, *Byronismo Italiano* (Milan, Casa Editrice L. F. Cogliati, 1923), pp. 45–62.

> Our sin the same, and hard as his to mend,
> Being Pride, which leads the mind to soar too far,
> Till our own weakness shows us what we are.   [IV.1]

What one immediately notices is the connection between this stanza and the imagery of flight we have met with in the Dedication. One thinks particularly of Blackbird Southey "overstraining" himself and "tumbling downwards like the flying fish," or even more, perhaps, of the ominous reference to the Tower of Babel. Here again a fall results from the attempt at a flight beyond one's proper powers. And, indeed, the motif is recurrent throughout the poem. At the beginning of Canto XI, for example, Byron describes the "spirit," some of whose metaphysical flights he had been discussing, as a liquor (a "draught," "Heaven's brandy") which is a bit too heady for the "brain" (XI.1). Metaphysical speculation is a kind of drunkenness, and the image is one of genial diminution. Then, with a characteristically Byronic modulation of the image of "indisposition," he adds:

> For ever and anon comes Indigestion
> (Not the most "dainty Ariel"), and perplexes
> Our soarings with another kind of question.   [XI.3]

Man's loftiest flights are subject to the unpredictable activities of the digestive system. (The further modulation of the image in stanzas 5 and 6, by which physical ills, just now seen as hazards to spiritual flight, become incentives to religious orthodoxy, strikes me as adroit.) The passage is only one of many emphasizing man's physical nature and the folly of forgetting it or trying to pretend that it is other than it is.

But both the stanza on poets and the lines on metaphysics differ in at least one important way from those passages in the Dedication which also make use of the image of flight. In the Dedication, while the satire is not merely personal, it does take the form of an attack on a real individual or group. This is a common device of satire, and one which Byron continues to use throughout the poem. But in *Don Juan* the satiric implications of the image are characteristically generalized. It is "we" who fall, and it is *"our* soarings" that are perplexed. Byron is making a comment on human beings in general, on human nature. And if the comment is not remarkably optimistic, neither is it broodingly grim.

The point is of particular importance with regard to the first passage ("Nothing so difficult, etc."). For what Byron is speaking of here is not merely a quality of bad poets; it is something that he sees as characteristic of *all* poets, including himself. A poet, to earn the name, *must* sometimes soar. How seriously he takes this may be seen from one of his most extended (and savage) attacks on Wordsworth. As usual, in order to appreciate properly a particular passage of *Don Juan,* it is necessary to see how it fits its context. The passage in question, stanzas 98–100 of Canto III, stands as the climax of a variation on one of the most important themes of the poem, the social significance of language (cf. the Dedication). The section has been initiated with the song of the island laureate, "The Isles of Greece." Here poetry is fulfilling its proper function (as it does not, we are told, in the case of Laureate Southey), serving the real interests of society rather than merely flattering its rulers. For

> . . . words are things, and a small drop of ink,
>   Falling like dew, upon a thought, produces
> That which makes thousands, perhaps millions, think.
>   [III.88]

Furthermore, in order to fulfill its social function poetry must be socially accessible. Hence the relevance of the attacks on Wordsworth's obscurity:

He there [in the *Excursion*] builds up a formidable dyke
Between his own and others' intellect.   [III.95]

These, then, are the most important considerations lying
behind the stanzas on Wordsworth with which the section
concludes:

We learn from Horace, "Homer sometimes sleeps;"
    We feel without him,—Wordsworth sometimes wakes,—
To show with what complacency he creeps
    With his dear *"Waggoners,"* around his lakes.
He wishes for "a boat" to sail the deeps—
    Of Ocean?—No, of air; and then he makes
Another outcry for "a little boat,"
And drivels seas to set it well afloat.

If he must fain sweep o'er the ethereal plain,
    And Pegasus runs restive in his "Waggon,"
Could he not beg the loan of Charles's Wain?
    Or pray Medea for a single dragon?
Or if, too classic for his vulgar brain,
    He feared his neck to venture such a nag on,
And he must needs mount nearer to the moon,
Could not the blockhead ask for a balloon?

"Pedlars," and "Boats," and "Waggons!" Oh! ye shades
    Of Pope and Dryden, are we come to this?
That trash of such sort not alone evades
    Contempt, but from the bathos' vast abyss
Floats scumlike uppermost, and these Jack Cades
    Of sense and song above your graves may hiss—
The "little boatman" and his *Peter Bell*
Can sneer at him who drew "Achitophel!"   [III.98–100]

The first complaint made about Wordsworth is that he
not only does not soar, he creeps. And he creeps around
lakes, permitting Byron to emphasize his alleged provinciality and limitation by repeating the lake-ocean contrast of

the Dedication. But this lake-ocean contrast is present only by implication in the explicit ocean-air contrast. While any flight is necessarily through the air, Byron is here taking advantage of its associations of triviality and bluff in order to discredit the flight of a poet whose characteristic motion is that of creeping around lakes. Byron's playing with the common Scriblerian notion of the proximity of the high and the low is brought out even more clearly by the highly Swiftian comments on the scum floating to the top "from the bathos' vast abyss."

But the satirist is also offended at the vehicle chosen for the poet's flight—"a little boat." There is something essentially improper, apparently, in a poet's soaring off in a boat, especially a little one. Perhaps he feels the symbol too private (cf. the final contrast between the fanciful *Peter Bell* and the public, socially relevant "Achitophel"), or, perhaps merely childish. It is not, at any rate, a proper bardic conveyance. Real poets ride the winged horse Pegasus (a persistent image in *Don Juan,* and an important one). Wordsworth's choice of a little boat, the satirist suggests, is a tacit admission of poetic inadequacy. Pegasus is far too spirited a steed for him: "He feared his neck to venture such a nag on."

In contrast to the creeping and floating of Wordsworth, the satirist bends and soars. The first refers to the natural gesture of the truthful muse, who is scrupulous in following her sources:

> A brave Tartar Khan—
> Or "Sultan," as the author (to whose nod
> In prose I bend my humble verse) doth call
> This chieftain—somehow would not yield at all.
>
> [VIII.104]

And this is no means the only time that we shall be reminded of the famous couplet from the "Epistle to Dr. Arbuthnot":

That not in Fancy's Maze he wander'd long,
But stoop'd to Truth, and moraliz'd his song.

[ll. 340–1]

In contrast both with the creeping and floating Wordsworth and the bending of the satiric muse is the soaring
poet of the beginning of Canto x:

In the wind's eye I have sailed, and sail; but for
    The stars, I own my telescope is dim;
But at the least I have shunned the common shore,
    And leaving land far out of sight, would skim
The Ocean of Eternity: the roar
    Of breakers has not daunted my slight, trim,
But *still* sea-worthy skiff; and she may float
Where ships have foundered, as doth many a boat.

[x.4]

One notices first of all the elements common to this stanza
and the section on Wordsworth. Here again there is flight
described in terms of floating in a boat. But what were there
images of contempt are here images expressive of a disarm-
ing modesty (an old rhetorical shift particularly valuable to
the satirist, whose pose inevitably implies pretensions of
personal merit). To be sure, he presents himself as an explorer of the Ocean (cf. the ocean–lake contrast) of Eternity, but then he owns that he has no very clear view of the
stars, and that his "slight, trim, / But *still* sea-worthy skiff"
merely "skims" the ocean, floating on its surface. It is important to notice that while he makes no very extravagant
claims as to his discoveries on the "Ocean of Eternity," he
does claim some credit for having undertaken the voyage.
He even asserts that it is of social (or generally human) utility, a point to which we shall return.

We are now perhaps in a position to profit from another
look at the passage from which we set out:

Nothing so difficult as a beginning
   In poesy, unless perhaps the end;
For oftentimes when Pegasus seems winning
   The race, he sprains a wing, and down we tend,
Like Lucifer, when hurled from Heaven for sinning;
   Our sin the same, and hard as his to mend,
Being Pride, which leads the mind to soar too far,
Till our own weakness shows us what we are.   [IV. 1]

The passage is, as I shall try to show, a particularly clear
statement of one version of the poem's central paradox. For
the moment it is enough to see how Byron is complicating
the traditional images of flight and fall. It is not merely that
the satirist's attacks on particular kinds of poetry and particular literary figures are elements in a more general criticism of a particular state of society (as the island Laureate
puts it: "The heroic lay is tuneless now— / The heroic
bosom beats no more!"). But Byron has associated the poetic
"flight" with diabolic pride, and he means it. Whatever may
have been his own personal convictions regarding the myth
of the war in heaven, it serves the poet as an indispensable
metaphor for some concepts and attitudes which seem to
have been very important to him and which are of central
importance for a proper understanding of his greatest poem.
The movement of the thought is roughly as follows: to be a
poet is a fine and valuable thing; poets, to be worthy the
name, must essay the grand manner (soar); but soaring is a
manifestation of the prime sin. It is this kind of paradox
that Byron's reading of the myth of the Fall is designed to
sustain and justify.

Byron most commonly, however, plays with the notion of
fall in terms of the Fall of Man:

We have
Souls to save, since Eve's slip and Adam's fall,

> Which tumbled all mankind into the grave,
> Besides fish, beasts, and birds.   [IX.19]

We have here at the very least an admission of man's radical imperfection, presented in terms of the Christian myth. Eve slipped,[4] Adam fell, and mankind became subject to death. And—this is very important—not mankind alone. "Fish, beasts, and birds" shared the curse of death placed on our First Parents. Nature, too, fell.[5] We live in a fallen world.

This fact may help explain Byron's notoriously ambiguous attitude toward the arts of civilization. They are at one time emblems of man's degeneration from an original paradisal state; at another they embody high human values. We are told, for example, that Haidée

> . . . was one
> Fit for the model of a statuary
>   (A race of mere impostors, when all's done—
> I've seen much finer women, ripe and real,
> Than all the nonsense of their stone ideal).
>
>   [II.118]

And of the Sultana we learn that she was "so beautiful that Art could little mend her" (VI.89). Here, of course, there is the implication that whatever might be true of Gulbeyaz, there are women whom art might conceivably improve. But then we are told, with reference to Juan's dress uniform at the court of Catherine the Great, that "Nature's self turns paler, / Seeing how Art can make her work more grand" (IX.44). The statements, taken in themselves, are clearly contradictory. But again this is not indecision or confusion. Not only do both points of view have their validity, but Byron supplies us with a consistent metaphor in terms of which the

---

4. Cf. Canto VI.94, where we are told that "one Lady's slip . . . [left] a crime on / All generations."

5. Cf. Lovell, esp. pp. 126–7. Lovell's whole discussion of Byron's attitude toward nature should be consulted.

fact may be contemplated. That basis is again the Christian myth of the Fall.

Four stanzas preceding the last passage quoted, Byron writes of the new Fall of Man that will occur when, according to Cuvier, the earth will next undergo one of its periodic convulsions and a new world is formed (Byron seems to think temptation integral to creation, and fall the inevitable consequence of temptation). He speaks with some compassion of

> . . . these young people, just thrust out
> From some fresh Paradise, and set to plough,
> And dig, and sweat, and turn themselves about,
> And plant, and reap, and spin, and grind, and sow,
> Till all the arts at length are brought about,
> Especially of War and taxing.   [ix.40]

The development of the arts of civilization, of which the art of poetry is exemplary, is clearly a consequence of the Fall, part of the taint of Original Sin.

I have thus far been stressing the negative side of the paradox. It is time now to imitate the poet himself and shift the emphasis to the positive pole. This change in emphasis may conveniently be considered with regard to the four beautifully modulated octaves with which Byron opens Canto x. He is here making explicit the mythic presuppositions in terms of which he is proceeding:

> When Newton saw an apple fall, he found
>   In that slight startle from his contemplation—
> 'Tis *said* (for I'll not answer above ground
>   For any sage's creed or calculation)—
> A mode of proving that the Earth turned round
>   In a most natural whirl, called "gravitation;"
> And this is the sole mortal who could grapple,
> Since Adam—with a fall—or with an apple.

Man fell with apples, and with apples rose,
     If this be true; for we must deem the mode
In which Sir Isaac Newton could disclose
     Through the then unpaved stars the turnpike road,
A thing to counterbalance human woes:
     For ever since immortal man hath glowed
With all kinds of mechanics, and full soon
Steam-engines will conduct him to the moon.   [x.1–2]

The concluding couplet of the first octave suggests that ever since the Fall of Adam man has suffered from a lack, a something wanting or a something wrong, with which Newton was the first successfully to contend. The reference is, of course, to the traditional notion of aberrations entering into a perfect creation with the Fall of Man, the crown of creation. Man, who in his paradisal state had ruled all things, now becomes subject to the vicissitudes of a fallen natural order. Byron sees a symbol of this state of subjection in natural man's helplessness before the law of gravity. The idea of fall, then, which we have already examined in connection with the Scriblerian concept of bathos, is here given much greater range by being associated with the force which in the physics of Byron's day was regarded as the governing principle of the natural order. As Byron sees it, since the Fall men naturally fall (morally and physically). The imaginative concept is very close to Simone Weil's notion of sin: "When . . . a man turns away from God, he simply gives himself up to the law of gravity." [6]

The second octave is most explicit: "Man fell with apples, and with apples rose." In a celebrated passage of his journal Baudelaire observes that true civilization "does not consist in gas or steam or turn-tables. It consists in the diminution

6. *Waiting for God*, tr. Emma Craufurd (New York, Putnam, 1951), p. 128. Could there be an echo of the imagery of the first of the *Holy Sonnets* here? Simone Weil knew the metaphysicals, and the whole section (of "The Love of God and Affliction") is filled with Donnean concepts and images.

of the traces of Original Sin." [7] But while Byron would probably not argue with this definition of civilization, his own views are rather more catholic. In his eyes gas and steam and turn-tables are legitimate and even important means for "the diminution of the traces of Original Sin." They are civilization's way of contending with and rising above a fallen nature. Scientific advance of the kind represented by Newton is "A thing to counterbalance human woes." And while there is mild irony in the picture of immortal man glowing over his gadgets and his steam engine to the moon, Byron's awareness of absurdity is clearly a complicating rather than a negating element.

Yet Byron is not merely (or even principally) interested in scientific advance. The art he is most concerned with is, as we have seen, the art of poetry:

> And wherefore this exordium?—Why, just now,
>   In taking up this paltry sheet of paper,
> My bosom underwent a glorious glow,
>   And my internal spirit cut a caper:
> And though so much inferior, as I know,
>   To those who, by the dint of glass and vapour,
> Discover stars, and sail in the wind's eye,
> I wish to do as much by Poesy.
>
> In the wind's eye I have sailed, and sail; but for
>   The stars, I own my telescope is dim;
> But at the least I have shunned the common shore,
>   And leaving land far out of sight, would skim
> The Ocean of Eternity: the roar
>   Of breakers has not daunted my slight, trim,

7. *Mon Cœur mis à nu*, sec. 59. I am using the translation in Peter Quennell, ed., *The Essence of Laughter* (New York, Meridian, 1956), p. 189. Robert Escarpit, in his ambitious *Lord Byron. Un Tempérament littéraire* (2 vols. Paris, Le Cercle du Livre, 1955), *1*, 153–61, makes a similar point with regard to the position adopted by Byron in his letters attacking William Lisle Bowles. But the Frenchman quotes Chesterton.

But *still* sea-worthy skiff; and she may float
Where ships have foundered, as doth many a boat.

[x.3–4]

We have met this last stanza before. Here the poet, who has been discussing scientific investigation, applies the image of exploration to his own pursuit. If Newton was an explorer, so too in his modest way is he.[8] This is a corollary to what he has said about the necessity of poetic "flight," the social utility of poetry, and the importance of a poet's rising above provinciality. The poet, who has been speaking of how science helps repair the faults in nature that arose as a result of the Fall, announces that it is his aim "to do the same by Poesy." Poetry too, then, is being seen as not merely emotional relief (though it is that) or relief from ennui (though it is that too), but "A thing to counterbalance human woes," an agent of civilization in its struggle for "the diminution of the traces of Original Sin."

The point is made only slightly less explicitly in the first two stanzas of Canto vii:

O Love! O Glory! what are ye who fly
    Around us ever, rarely to alight?
There's not a meteor in the polar sky
    Of such transcendent and more fleeting flight.
Chill, and chained to cold earth, we lift on high
    Our eyes in search of either lovely light;

8. Exploration as a metaphor for poetic activity occurs more than once. In xiv.101, for example, in a passage we shall be examining later (below, p. 110), the poet observes that

The new world would be nothing to the old,
    If some Columbus of the moral seas
    Would show mankind their souls' antipodes.

Or again (xv.27):

We [i.e. "my Muse" and I] surely may find something worth research:
    Columbus found a new world in a cutter, etc.

The image is basic to *Childe Harold*.

A thousand and a thousand colours they
Assume, then leave us on our freezing way.

And such as they are, such my present tale is,
    A nondescript and ever-varying rhyme,
A versified Aurora Borealis,
    Which flashes o'er a waste and icy clime.
When we know what all are, we must bewail us,
    But ne'ertheless I hope it is no crime
To laugh at *all* things—for I wish to know
What, after *all,* are *all* things—but a *show?*

[VII.1–2]

The claims here are rather more modest, but the principle is the same. Byron's "wasteland" symbol is that of a frozen world. Since Byron sometimes believed in Cuvier's theory of periodic destruction and recreation of the earth, and since on at least one occasion he conceived the annihilation of life on our world as the result of freezing (in the fragment "Darkness"), he may be thinking of a kind of progressive chill leading to final annihilation. At any rate the "icy clime" is not a cultural wasteland. It is presented rather as a state natural to man, an inevitable symbol of a fallen world. Man is "chained to cold earth" (like Prometheus on "icy Caucasus") [9] and is able to alleviate his sufferings only by his own efforts—by love and glory and, as we learn in the second stanza, by poetry. This very poem is presented as an attempt to give color, form, warmth to a world naturally colorless, indefinite, and chill.

The poem, like the meteor, exercises a double function. First of all, it sheds light ("flashes o'er a waste and icy clime"), the light that reveals the rather grim truth about the state of man on earth ("when we know what all are, we must bewail us"). But the poem, even while revealing the melancholy state of man, helps him to come to terms

9. Cf. Bloom, *Shelley's Mythmaking,* pp. 91–2.

with it. The act of exposing the sad reality exposes the absurdity of the pretense that it is otherwise, while providing through art a means of dealing with it without the hypocrisy and self-deception integral to Love and Glory:

> Dogs, or men!—for I flatter you in saying
>> That ye are dogs—your betters far—ye may
> Read, or read not, what I am now essaying
>> To show ye what ye are in every way.
> As little as the moon stops for the baying
>> Of wolves, will the bright Muse withdraw one ray
> From out her skies—then howl your idle wrath!
> While she still silvers o'er your gloomy path.   [VII.7]

This I take to be the true rationale behind the alleged "cynicism" of *Don Juan*. It is thus a prime expression of the positive pole of the paradox whose negative aspects we have already examined.

The argument thus far, then, would run something as follows. Byron, in developing the world of *Don Juan,* makes use of the Christian concepts of sin, fall, and the fallen state. He is writing a poem in terms of such a world. The poem is presumably going to be of help with regard to man's fallen condition. But at the same time, like all products of civilization, the act of writing poetry holds in itself the danger of fall. It inevitably implies, for example, participation in the original sin of pride and revolt. Or, to reverse the emphasis (as Byron does), there is "evil" in art, but there is also a good which can help at least to overcome the evil. And this paradox is based on a still profounder one, a vision of the radically paradoxical nature of "the way things are"—that is, of nature itself. For, as we have seen, in the world of *Don Juan* nature is fallen and stands in need of redemption. And at the same time, nature is valuable both in itself and as a norm against which a corrupt civilization may be exposed. For the Christian, nature is fallen and must be redeemed. But though fallen, nature is God's creation and must of necessity retain the imprint of the Creator (hence the possibility of "natural theology").

The practical importance of close attention to this paradoxical nature of both art and nature is evident when one comes to consider an episode such as the banquet at Norman Abbey (xv.62–74). Even so useful a critic as Truman Guy Steffan, for example, has permitted himself to dismiss the episode as a kind of tour de force whose only function is "to make his point about fastidious elegance, conspicuous waste, and the sodden dullness of gormandizing." [1] That there is something in this I should not attempt to deny. But an adequate reading of this brilliant episode would reveal something rather more interesting. It is satire, of course, but it is not merely satire. And as satire it is more in the vein of *The Rape of the Lock* than of Juvenal's Fourth, which is what Steffan's rather grim description calls to mind.

The opening lines, in fact, seem almost like a deliberate reminiscence of Pope's mock epic—the Invocation, perhaps, or the game of ombre:

> Great things were now to be achieved at table,
>   With massy plate for armour, knives and forks
> For weapons.   [xv.62]

The poet explicitly reminds us of the feasts in Homer. But the most relevant literary connection is with the satiric tradition. In both Horace and Juvenal (to say nothing of Petronius) meals are used as symbols of social values. Social ideals and conditions, that is, are dramatized through the communal meal (the *cena*). Byron himself seems to be hinting at this with his mention of the turbot (63; it occurs again at the election dinner, xvi.88). For the turbot (*rhom-*

1. Steffan, *Variorum, 1,* 264. See also the admirable essay by Lovell, cited above, p. xiii n.

bus) is an almost indispensable part of the equipment of the satirist who is treating of social decay in terms of diet. Pope mentions it twice in his "imitation" of Horace's *Serm.* ii.ii.[2] It is almost as conventional as Pope's and Byron's mechanical references to the appetite of aldermen.

But Byron's dinner party is still more firmly traditional. His stanza 73, comparing the olives and wine of the elaborate feast with those he had eaten, "The grass for my table-cloth, in open air, / On Sunium or Hymettus," corresponds to Horace's and Pope's references to the place of simple olives at the gourmand's table (Horace, 45–6; Pope, 31–6), though the point is rather different. While Horace and his Augustan imitator are speaking "satirically," Byron is at least as interested in developing the *persona* as one who, as he has said of Juan, has "the art of living in all climes with ease" (xv.11). It is the sophistication of the speaker rather than moral indignation at the bill of fare at Norman Abbey that is most at issue here. The point is not a trivial one if the "moral" of *Don Juan* is to be sought in the suave ambivalences of attitude manifested by the speaker.

The episode we are considering is, from this point of view, particularly rich. Consider, for example, the following excerpt from the menu:

> Then there was God knows what "à l'Allemande,"
>   "A l'Espagnole," "timballe," and "salpicon"—
> With things I can't withstand or understand,
>   Though swallowed with much zest upon the whole;
> And *"entremets"* to piddle with at hand,
>   Gently to lull down the subsiding soul;
> While great Lucullus' *Robe triumphal* muffles—
> (*There's fame*)—young partridge fillets, decked with
>   truffles.   [xv.66]

2. Pope, ll. 23, 141. See Horace, *Serm.* ii.ii.42, 48, 49, 95; viii.30, or Juvenal, *Sat.* xi.121, and iv passim.

The first two lines remind us of the foreign nature of the feast. The dishes are French, and the references to "à l'Allemande" and "A l'Espagnole" heighten the meal's cosmopolitan character. This is not, as we are reminded in 71, "roast beef in our rough John Bull way." And while the speaker is clearly amused, there is hardly any suggestion that he seriously disapproves of such goings-on in the house of an English peer. He enjoys playing with the names just as he would, apparently, enjoy the meal—the dishes described are "things I can't withstand or understand." They are strange and amusing and irresistible to a *bonne vivante* Muse.

The reference to the *entremets* is especially interesting. They are things "to piddle with" in order "gently to lull down the subsiding soul." The tone here is remarkably bland when one considers the source of the allusion (which has apparently escaped the annotators). "Piddle" was one of Pope's words. He uses it, for example, in the same Horatian imitation mentioned above (II.ii.137). Further, and more significantly, the expression "subsiding soul" is clearly derived from this same poem, where "The Soul subsides" is Pope's rendering of the Horatian "animum quoque praegravat" (Horace, 60; Pope, 79). And this, in turn, is the same passage to which Byron refers us in a gloss on his own "very fiery particle" stanza on the death of Keats (*Don Juan* XI.60). This is rather a lofty flight in Horace, and while it is less impressive in Pope's version, Byron is startlingly casual when compared with either of his sources. This is especially striking when one recalls that Byron thought food actually to have a lulling effect on his soul. One must watch the tone carefully. Byron is suggesting that the guests at Norman Abbey were dragging the mind down with the body and fastening a particle of the divine spirit to the earth. But there is little to hint that this is anything worse than amusing. And when we are a little better ac-

quainted with Byron's Prometheanism we may understand
how the poet could speak so genially of acquiescing in the
power of the "clay."

At any rate, if Byron has any very grim denunciatory purposes in mind he makes very little of his opportunity. He
moves on immediately to another theme, exploiting the
fact that Lucullus had been a successful general as well as a
gourmand. Both in a prose note and in stanza 67 Byron en-
larges on the superiority of culinary to military glory.
"What are the *fillets* on the Victor's brow / To these?" [3]
Perhaps the lines on the great things to be achieved at table
were not merely facetious.

We have seen something of how Byron tends to interject
allusions to the Fall of Man at strategic points in *Don Juan;*
and the dinner party is no exception:

> The mind is lost in mighty contemplation
>   Of intellect expanded on two courses;
> And Indigestion's grand multiplication
>   Requires arithmetic beyond my forces.
> Who would suppose, from Adam's simple ration,
>   That cookery could have called forth such resources,
> As form a science and a nomenclature
> From out the commonest demands of Nature?   [xv.69]

The stanza begins with an ironic expression of awe at the
vast quantity of intellectual energy expended on devising a
meal such as this. There is something magnificent about

3. Cf. 1.128–34. Here, where there is an ambivalence of attitude similar to
that found in the stanzas on the dinner, Byron observes that "Vaccination
certainly has been / A kind antithesis to Congreve's rockets" (129), and that

> Sir Humphry Davy's lantern, by which coals
> Are safely mined for in the mode he mentions,
>   Tombuctoo travels, voyages to the Poles
> Are ways to benefit mankind, as true,
> Perhaps, as shooting them at Waterloo.   [132]

it. But intellect so employed leads (according to the laws of physiology and assonance) to an indigestion of still greater sublimity. For it is as true of cookery as of poetry that pride "leads the mind to soar too far, / Till our own weakness shows us what we are" (IV.1). And in neither case is the attitude toward the presumption of the artist, poet or cook, quite a simple one. For example, the last four lines of the stanza quoted above contrast the artifice of Norman Abbey with the dietary simplicity of (presumably prelapsarian) Adam. Man's actual needs are few and excess is comic. But Byron does not seem disposed merely to "reason the need." If the *"goût"* leads to the "gout" (72), it is still a refinement of nature. There is art involved, and ingenuity. The poet smiles, but he also appreciates. The versifier of a cookbook is not a man to scorn a tour de force. Luxury, again, is a result of the Fall—but in a way it is one of man's means of dealing with the conditions brought about by the Fall. And again, the emphasis is being placed on the second element, the positive pole of the paradox the poet is engaged in defining.

One can see, then, how essential it is to come to a clear understanding of Byron's attitude towards nature, one that has more in common with Baudelaire than with Rousseau. We think, for example, of his allusion to "ruts, and flints, and lovely Nature's skill" (IX.31), referring to a post road insufficiently refined by art. Or again, at the Battle of Ismail, there seems to be no great moral gain when "the Art of War," however dubious an achievement of civilization, is replaced by "human nature":

> Death is drunk with gore: there's not a street
> Where fights not to the last some desperate heart
>   For those for whom it soon shall cease to beat.
> Here War forgot his own destructive art
>   *In more destroying Nature;* and the heat

Of Carnage, like the Nile's sun-sodden slime,
Engendered monstrous shapes of every crime.

[VIII.82; my italics] [4]

The real horror of war is the result not of civilization but of
the natural fallen heart of man. The human "clay" (a favorite metaphor), when exposed to "the heat / Of Carnage,"
naturally brings forth "monstrous shapes of every crime."
It is as natural for human nature to react to the circumstances of a battlefield with "sub-human" brutality as it is
for monsters to be produced from the ooze of the Nile. But
the social order is at least largely responsible for the circumstances. This is what Byron is reminding us when he asks,
with reference to the Cossacks pursuing the child Leila:

And whom for this at last must we condemn?
Their natures? or their sovereigns, who employ
All arts to teach their subjects to destroy?   [VIII.92]

Again, this seems an attitude which it is hardly fair to dismiss as either oversimple or confused.

Of these same Cossacks the poet has observed:

Matched with *them,*
The rudest brute that roams Siberia's wild
Has feelings pure and polished as a gem,—
The bear is civilised, the wolf is mild.   [*ibid.*]

The notion is a familiar one. Man has it in him to be
worse than the worst of the beasts if he gives in to his lower
instincts. As Juan himself puts it when he refuses to give
the crew of the sinking ship access to the grog: "Let us die
like men, not sink below / Like brutes" (II.36). For when
the ship goes down, carring with it the appurtenances of

4. Cf. Selim's comment on the savagery of his band (*Bride of Abydos,* ll.
910–11):

Yet there we follow but the bent assigned
By *fatal Nature* to man's warring kind.   [my italics]

civilization, and passengers and crew are set adrift on the
sea (whose symbolic suggestions in this connection should
be clear enough), man has an admirable opportunity for
showing what his nature is.[5] It is not surprising, therefore,
that in this episode the poet should make good use of animal imagery.

We are told, for example, that "like the shark and tiger
[man] must have prey" (67). And though Juan had at first
declined to join in eating his father's spaniel, he finally gives
in when he feels "all the vulture in his jaws" (71). Again,
after seven days under a scorching sun on a windless sea,
thoughts of cannibalism are to be seen "in their wolfish
eyes" (72). Finally, when the men draw lots to decide who
is to be eaten, we are told: " 'Twas Nature gnawed them to
this resolution" (75). The suggestion seems to be that nature is a beast that seeks to reduce man to its level. This is
the same malicious nature we have met only a few stanzas
before, where the sea is compared to

> . . . a veil,
> Which, if withdrawn, would but disclose the frown
> Of one whose hate is masked but to assail.   [II.49]

Nature lures man on with its beauty and its apparent calm,
then shows itself in its true savagery. It is this meal (on
Pedrillo) and this nature that should be borne in mind as
we read of the elaborately "unnatural" banquet at Norman
Abbey.

But the shipwreck episode, though less subtle than the
banquet scene, is not so simple as is sometimes suggested.
The matter-of-fact tone, reminiscent of Swift, may help keep
the episode, unsparing as it is, from impressing one as the
product of a morbid misanthropy. If it is possible for man to
act this way, it is well perhaps to acknowledge the fact. It
would be questionable only if the poet were suggesting

5. Cf. Steffan, p. 192.

that the cannibals in the long-boat were an adequate embodiment of what man "really" is. Byron, at least, is not
so naive. He is no more suggesting that man is "really" a
beast than is Goya in the brutish figures of the *Caprichos*.
In both cases the bestial is seen as an aberration from a
human norm suggested in the drawings by the prefatory
figure of the wide-awake and fully rational artist [6] and in
the poem by the complex rationality of the ever-present
speaker. Furthermore, the hero himself is carefully pre-
served from falling completely into animality. He has no
part in the cannibalism, and is reluctant even to eat the
spaniel's paw. It must be remembered, moreover, that the
episode is only one part of a rather long poem; it enjoys
no unique authority. Finally, there is in passages such as
the following a note of what can almost be called admiration for the sheer toughness of human beings, their ability
to hang on to life in the most difficult circumstances:

> 'Tis thus with people in an open boat,
>   They live upon the love of Life, and bear
> More than can be believed, or even thought,
>   And stand like rocks the tempest's wear and tear;
> And hardship still has been the sailor's lot,
>   Since Noah's ark went cruising here and there.
>
> [II.66]

This feeling for the fineness amidst the meanness of human life is central to Byron's vision in *Don Juan*.

Steffan has recently commented on the contrast between
the storm and shipwreck and the Haidée episode. This contrast, he suggests, is the structural basis of Canto II. In the
stanzas on the shipwreck nature is seen in its grim, and in

---

6. Cf. José López-Rey, *Goya's Caprichos* (2 vols. Princeton Univ. Press,
1953), *1*, 75–8.

the Haidée episode in its cheerful, aspect.[7] Though the contrast is clear enough, we might note briefly one of the ways in which it is dramatized. I have already commented on the use of animal imagery in the shipwreck episode. There the images were of sharks, vultures, wolves. Here the characteristic image is of birds. Haidée's voice, for example, "was the warble of a bird" (II.151). Every morning she would come to the cave "To see her bird reposing in his nest" (II.168). At the consummation of their love she "flew to her young mate like a young bird" (II.190). The two lovers speak their own language, "like to that of birds" (IV.14). Further, "there was no reason for their loves / More than for those of nightingales or doves" (IV.19). And they are by implication the "sweetest song-birds" of IV.28. Birds seem to be a Byronic symbol of natural innocence and beauty (cf. Immalee in Maturin's *Melmoth*) in contrast with the earlier animal symbols of natural depravity. Both are part of Byron's vision.

But while it is easy enough to see the point of the usual generalizations about the idyllic life on the isle, it might be well to try to define certain aspects of it a little more closely. One thinks, for example, of the violence of which Juan comes to the isle in the first place. The only survivor of a savage storm on a treacherous ocean, he is washed up on a shore not conspicuously hospitable (II.104): "The shore looked wild, without a trace of man, / And girt by formidable waves." There are "roaring breakers," "A reef," "boiling surf and bounding spray." Shipwrecks, further, are not uncommon on this coast. Haidée made a fire

> . . . with such
> Materials as were cast up round the bay,—
> Some broken planks, and oars, that to the touch

7. Cf. Steffan, pp. 193-4.

    Were nearly tinder, since, so long they lay,
      A mast was almost crumbled to a crutch;
    But, by God's grace, here wrecks were in such plenty,
      That there was fuel to have furnished twenty.   [II.132]

And while we learn that there is a port "on the other side
o' the isle" (III.19), it is the "shoal and bare" coast with its
treacherous reefs and currents that is most impressed upon
us.[8]

The point is worth mentioning if for no other reason
than that, as Byron is careful to point out, it is here, on a
coast whose perils have been repeatedly emphasized, that
the peculiarly harmonious and ideal love of Juan and
Haidée is consummated:

    Amidst the barren sand and rocks so rude
    She and her wave-worn love had made their bower.
                                                [II.198]

Now the violent sea that had wrecked Juan's ship and which
beats upon the shore "spills" a "small ripple" on the beach,
like "the cream of your champagne" (II.178). More, these
same storms that cost the lives of Juan's shipmates create
beauty as they work on the hard rock of the coast. They
smooth the pebbles of the beach so that they shine in the
moonlight, and they form "hollow halls, with sparry roofs
and cells," in one of which Juan and Haidée "turned to
rest" (II.184).

More is involved here than the traditional motif of
"beauty in the lap of horror." This is a particularly fine
expression of one of the most important qualities of
Haidée's isle. It is a place where natural violence is tem-
pered to beauty, but where the violence forms an indispensable basis to the beauty created. There is, for exam-

8. Lovell (p. 206) has called attention to the inhospitable terrain of
Haidée's isle, though for a different reason.

ple, the famous "fancy piece" of the "band of children, round a snow-white ram," wreathing "his venerable horns with flowers" (III.32). Or, more importantly, there is Lambro himself (for it is properly *his* island), the violence of his nature and his life, and the kind of ideal existence made possible by this violence (and which corresponds to another aspect of his nature). For on the simplest level one can hardly ignore the rather dubious economic basis of the island pastoral. Juan and Haidée's idyllic, natural existence, surrounded by slaves, tapestries, fine Persian carpets, and sherbets chilled in porous vessels, is, after all, supported by a career of piracy and murder. This is too simple, of course, since the important point is the use the two lovers make of their opportunities. They dine (and one should bear their by no means austere buffet in mind also when one considers the banquet at Norman Abbey) and dress and move among their luxurious surroundings with a consecrating grace. But this is precisely what I mean. There is no real irony in the vulgar sense. Byron is not so crude as to say, "Yes, Juan and Haidée live beautifully, but look at the evil and violence that supports their existence." It is rather the other way around; he would say, "Yes, Lambro is a man of violence (as nature is violent), but Lambro makes possible the creation of beauty (just as the violence of nature may make beauty)." And this is more than an especially accomplished development of the paradoxes implicit in the relations of art and nature. It looks ahead to the English cantos (cf. the banquet scene already discussed), where this attitude is given definitive expression.

And as violence and disorder lurk behind the most winning manifestations of tranquillity and harmony, the tranquil and harmonious are fated inevitably to dissolve again in the violent and chaotic. This is an apparently immutable law of Byron's world. Haidée was, we are told, "Nature's bride" (II.202), and the love she shared with Juan is explicitly contrasted in its naturalness with the unnatural situation of woman in society (199–201). Their union is a kind of act of natural religion:

> She loved, and was belovéd—she adored,
>   And she was worshipped after Nature's fashion.
>
>   [II.191]

The completeness of their commitment to and involvement in the processes of nature is dramatized in a rather flashy piece of romantic mingling:

> They looked up to the sky, whose floating glow
>   Spread like a rosy Ocean, vast and bright;
> They gazed upon the glittering sea below,
>   Whence the broad Moon rose circling into sight;
> They heard the waves' splash, and the wind so low,
>   And saw each other's dark eyes darting light
> Into each other.   [II.185]

It is a twilight moment (184) when daylight distinctions are blurred and all nature seems one.[9] The sky as they look at it seems a glowing sea, while the ocean itself is a night sky with the moon rising. The sound of the waves mingles

---

9. Byron is fond of this twilight motif, which serves so effectively as a metaphor of the peace, harmony, and wholeness to be found in nature. It is the hour sacred to Juan and Haidée (IV.20), in whom one important aspect of this natural harmony is manifested, and he celebrates it in one of the best-known purple patches in the poem (III.101–9). The poet, who in the previous stanzas (III.94–100) has been attacking Wordsworth for the private nature, the obscurity, and the provinciality of his verse, lovingly endows his own twilight meditation with a wealth of socially accessible allusion. We have two stanzas of sentimental Catholicism (102–3), one of eighteenth-century pantheism (104), references to the literary associations of the Pineta at Ravenna (105–6), and paraphrases of the evening hymns of Sappho and Dante (107 and 108). Byron makes especially effective use of the ambiguities of the image to dramatize the "fall" of Juan and Haidée, reminding us that twilight can not only dramatize oneness, but can also express a close, an ending of something valuable ("the descending sun" of IV.22). It is a useful type of the paradoxical nature of nature in Byron's vision.

with the sound of the wind. And just as the sky seemed to float like a sea and as the sea bore a moon like the sky, the "dark eyes" of the two lovers darted "light / Into each other." They mingle as sea and sky mingle, natural phenomena among natural phenomena.

But it is precisely because of the completeness of their harmony with nature that they are not exempt from sharing in its less idyllic manifestations. Such involvement in the natural, while it makes possible something so beautiful as the love of the two young "birds," implies also a participation in the vicissitudes inevitable to a fallen nature, particularly in its subjection to mutability:

> The Heart is like the sky, a part of Heaven,
> But changes night and day, too, like the sky;
> Now o'er it clouds and thunder must be driven,
> And Darkness and Destruction as on high:
> But when it hath been scorched, and pierced, and riven,
> Its storms expire in water-drops; the eye
> Pours forth at last the Heart's blood turned to tears,
> Which make the English climate of our years.   [II.214]

While this is primarily an explanation of Juan's unfaithfulness to Julia, it is presented as a general truth applicable to all men. The heart is traditionally that part of us which is most "natural" and which is valued (or distrusted) for that reason. Byron is trying to make clear exactly what is implied in the notion of "natural man." That involvement in the natural which is from one point of view an ideal is from another point of view part of the burden of fallen man, "given up to the law of gravity."

It has been suggested above how much the natural love of Juan and Haidée owes to Lambro, whose piratical career is presented as a metaphor of the real nature of the activities of great men in the great world.[1] But that civilization must at the same time take much of the blame for the idyll's

1. See esp. III.14.

violent dissolution is made quite explicit.[2] Civilization has from one point of view enhanced the idyll, and from another point of view it has contributed to its destruction. As Elizabeth Boyd has observed in this connection: "Evil is inherent in the nature of man; he does not have to learn it from society, though society frequently succeeds in first evoking it."[3] And the hideous effect of this double evil, natural and social, is seen in the death of Haidée.

We have previously seen Haidée's innocent heart heavenly "like the sky." Now we must see it "scorched, and pierced, and riven" by the storms of experience. In the dream that embodies the uneasiness of their last twilight rendezvous (IV.31–5), Haidée sees herself chained to one of the jagged cliffs of the shore. She has fallen from the paradise of the love idyll to the level of struggling humanity "Chill, and chained to cold earth." The "small ripple spilt upon the beach" (II.178) has become the "loud roar" of the rough waves rising to drown her (IV.31). The "shining pebbles" and the "smooth and hardened sand" of the pastoral (II.184) have become the "sharp shingles" that cut her feet as she pursues the terrifying something in a sheet that has replaced the seemingly secure reality of her love (IV.32). And the completeness of her (anticipated) union with the forces of nature is dramatized by her tears' joining them in their activity of forming marble icicles in a sea-cave strongly reminiscent of that to which she and Zoe had first borne the half-drowned Juan.[4]

2. See IV.28:

> They should have lived together deep in woods,
> > Unseen as sings the nightingale; they were
> Unfit to mix in these thick solitudes
> > Called social, haunts of Hate, and Vice, and Care.

3. Elizabeth French Boyd, *Byron's Don Juan. A Critical Study* (New Brunswick, Rutgers Univ. Press, 1945), p. 62.

4. Cf. the following:

> The fire burst forth from her Numidian veins,
> Even as the Simoom sweeps the blasted plains.   [IV.57]

Since it is essential that the implications of what has been suggested thus far be thoroughly grasped before going further, it may be well briefly to reiterate the main points toward which the argument has been moving and the kinds of relation it has been attempting to establish. I have already alluded to the general position in the Preface when I observed: "The underlying principle of Byron's universe seems to be that its elements are in their different ways both means of grace and occasions of sin." Now the religious image is misleading if one understands it in too moral a sense. The point is not that a thing is good if used properly and bad if used improperly. It simply *is* both good and bad. But it is *good* and *bad*. I make use of theological terminology because Byron does, and he does so because it is expressively necessary for him. The universe, as Byron sees it, is not merely inconveniently arranged, or not arranged at all and so humanly neutral. There is, from man's viewpoint at least, something profoundly wrong about it and about his place in it. But at the same time there is generous provision of means and opportunities of dealing with this wrongness and making it humanly right. But these means and opportunities have a way of being closely allied with the primary causes and manifestations of the wrongness. All this is not what *Don Juan* is about. It is about coming to terms with such a world. But something very like this is what *Don Juan* presupposes.

Examination of the poem makes it clear that the overt contrast between art and nature is in some ways less significant in the world of *Don Juan* than is the contrast be-

---

And:

> The tears rushed forth from her o'erclouded brain,
> Like mountain mists at length dissolved in rain.   [IV.66]

Coleridge (*Poetry, 6,* 192 n.) calls attention at this point to the cave in *The Island* (IV.121 ff.). A more useful analogue (or even "source") might be the cave in which Shelley's Cythna is imprisoned in *The Revolt of Islam* (VII.12–18).

tween the two aspects of either nature or art taken in themselves. Byron's nature, the authoritative embodiment of his notion of the way things are, is, like the Christian nature, a double one. It is beneficent and normative; and at the same time it is harsh and in need of correction and control. Byron appropriates the traditional paradox, adapting it to the purposes of his own paradoxical vision. Art, the conventional opposite to nature, reflects precisely the same duality. It is good in that it helps make a fallen world bearable; and it is bad in that it conspires to aggravate the condition of fall. Finally, there is love. And we shall find that love, the specific "matter" of *Don Juan,* shares also in this radical duality. This aspect of the paradox will be examined in the following chapter.

Chapter 3

"THE UNFORGIVEN FIRE"

IN CHAPTER 2 I tried to suggest something of what Byron seems to be doing with his references to the myth of the Fall, developing this in terms of his paradoxical attitude toward art and nature. But we should not forget that *Don Juan* is, after all, a poem about a great lover and that it deals largely with love.

An oblique approach is sometimes useful. Byron's psychology (and ethic) of the passions may be best approached by examining one of his shorter poems. I have in mind a curiously metaphysical piece called "Ode to a Lady whose Lover was killed by a ball, which at the same time shivered a Portrait next his Heart." It was first printed in 1901, when E. H. Coleridge, who got it "from an autograph MS. in the possession of Mr. Murray," included it in the fourth volume of his edition of Byron's poems. It is apparently unsigned and undated, and Coleridge gives no indication as to where or when it might have been written. Though I am not aware that there has ever been any question as to its authenticity, it seems at least possible that it is a translation of some Italian poem as yet unidentified. While I should like the poem to be original, whether it is or not is of no great importance for this study. If it is a translation, we may fairly assume that there was something about it that especially struck Byron so as to impel him to the labor of translation. Furthermore, if a translation, it is a remarkably accomplished piece of English versification, all the more remarkable because Byron's translations (with the notable exception of the Vittorelli sonnet) are apt to be stiff and awkward. The Ode has a rhythmic sophistication unsurpassed in Byron. But the important thing about it is that, original or translation, it is a brilliant, compressed expression of certain qualities of Byron's mature poetry which have still not received sufficient attention, and which find their most extended treatment in *Don Juan*.[1] In order to make this clear, it will be necessary to work through the poem with some care.

After a brief "Motto" from La Rochefoucauld ("On peut trouver des femmes qui n'ont jamais eu de galanterie, mais il est rare d'en trouver qui n'en aient jamais eu qu'une"),[2] the poem opens with a stately address to the Lady:

> Lady! in whose heroic port
> And Beauty, Victor even of Time,
>   And haughty lineaments, appear
>   Much that is awful, more that's dear—
>   Wherever human hearts resort
>   *There* must have been for thee a Court,
>   And Thou by acclamation Queen,
>   Where never Sovereign yet had been.

1. If by any wild chance the manuscript should turn out to be one of the "G. Byron" forgeries, I could only conclude that the forger's acknowledged genius for the centrally Byronic was even greater than has been realized.

2. Cf. *Don Juan*, III.4:

> Yet there are some [women], they say, who have had *none*,
> But those who have ne'er end with only *one*.

Or again, in the "Reply to Blackwood's *Edinburgh Magazine*" (*LJ, 4,* 488): "Writing grows a habit, like a woman's gallantry; there are women who have had no intrigue, but few who have had but one only."

The gracious dignity of the first three lines corresponds to those qualities of the Lady that are being stressed: her "haughty lineaments" and her "heroic port / And Beauty," which is seen as "Victor even of Time." [3] The qualifying "Victor even of Time" is placed so as to interrupt the sequence of attributes in order to retard the movement (adding to the stateliness of the lines), to emphasize the note of thoughtfulness, and, by bringing it forcibly to our attention, to prepare for its ironic qualification in the second stanza. In the fourth line both syntactical and rhetorical structures are resolved in the gracefully balanced subject: "Much that is awful, more that's dear." The balanced structure introduces, of course, a paradox. The "haughty" and "heroic" figure (with the martial implications of "Victor") is seen as, at the same time, "dear" (amiable, lovable). [4] "Wherever human hearts resort," the poet goes on, this amiability must have been recognized and cherished. But even this recognition on the part of the world at large insists on her quality of stateliness, for among men she is a "Queen," a "Sovereign," with her "Court" in human society. Furthermore, hers is a natural regality. It is acknowledged ("by acclamation") by men who had not hitherto made obeisance to any monarch. And finally, the passage looks forward both to the love with which the poem is principally concerned and to that of the "baffled" suitors in the last stanza.

> That eye so soft, and yet severe,
> > Perchance might look on Love as Crime;
> And yet—regarding thee more near—
> The traces of an unshed tear

3. I assume that "Victor even of Time" modifies both "port" and "Beauty": It makes better thematic sense that way. But it is just as easy syntactically to take it as referring to "Beauty" alone. With regard to the thought of the line see *Don Juan,* v.97–8.

4. The paradox will be discussed below with regard to the heroines of *Don Juan.*

Compressed back to the heart,
And mellowed Sadness in thine air,
Which shows that Love hath once been there,
To those who watch thee will disclose
More than ten thousand tomes of woes
    Wrung from the vain Romancer's art.

With the ninth line the poet restates the earlier paradox,
now in terms of her "eye so soft, and yet severe." The emphasis this time is reversed. Her eye is "soft," to be sure, but
its severity is such that one looking into it might suppose
that it is hardly an eye that would be susceptible to the
softer passions: it might well regard love itself as a crime
(ironic, in view of the "guilty" love to which she has surrendered). But then again, on closer inspection, the "traces
of an unshed tear" (Queens do not weep—not publicly, at
any rate) and a certain "mellowed Sadness" in her manner
(when Queens display their feelings it is with dignity) suggest to the man of the world that she has indeed known
love. Paradoxically, the very restraint with which her grief
is revealed makes it more eloquent than "ten thousand"
volumes of factitious romance.[5]

With thee how proudly Love hath dwelt!
His full Divinity was felt,
Maddening the heart he could not melt,
    Till Guilt became Sublime;
But never yet did Beauty's Zone
For him surround a lovelier throne,
Than in that bosom once his own:
    And he the Sun and Thou the Clime
Together must have made a Heaven
For which the Future would be given.

The paradox of love and pride attains a kind of resolution in the splendid verse: "With thee how proudly Love

5. Cf. comments on the romance theme in *Don Juan,* below, pp. 92 ff.

hath dwelt!" It is pride, indeed, but loving; or again, it is love, but proud. Regal creature that she is, gorgeous "throne" that she provides,[6] Love could find no fitter, no fairer palace than her breast, no more suitable temple in which to reveal his "full Divinity." And then again, nothing less than this full divinity could possibly influence one who is herself so proud, so queenly. "He the Sun and Thou the Clime," Love and the Lady together compose a Heaven for which all one's hopes for the future might properly be sacrificed (including, presumably, one's hopes for attaining to a more orthodox, Christian Heaven).

But even while the apparent resolution of the paradox is being so exquisitely celebrated, a darker note is receiving almost equal emphasis. Proud Love, faced with a heart so proud that it is not susceptible to his softer suasions, drives that heart to madness. It is the Lady's own almost superhuman dignity and control that, unable to bow to the storm as a lesser soul might have done, is violently broken by it. She falls to madness, to sin. But the very intensity of her guilt, of the passion to which she has so wholeheartedly surrendered, confers on it a kind of grandeur, a sublimity appropriate to such a woman.[7] Thus the first stanza ends on a complex note of triumph and tragedy.

2

And thou hast loved—Oh! not in vain!
And not as common Mortals love.
The Fruit of Fire is Ashes,
The Ocean's tempest dashes
Wrecks and the dead upon the rocky shore:

6. Cf. the image of Love "seated on his loveliest throne, / A sincere woman's breast" (*Don Juan*, vi.15).

7. Cf. Madame de Merteuil's comments on "that complete abandonment of self, that delirium of delight wherein pleasure is purified by its excess." Chaderlos de Laclos, *Les Liaisons dangereuses*, tr. Richard Aldington, *Dangerous Acquaintances* (Norfolk, New Directions, n.d.), p. 10 (Pt. I, Letter 5).

True Passion must the all-searching changes prove,
 The Agony of Pleasure and of Pain,
 Till Nothing but the Bitterness remain;
 And the Heart's Spectre flitting through the brain
Scoffs at the Exorcism which would remove.

The opening lines of the second stanza are especially dense. The Lady, we are told, has not loved "in vain." On one level, her love was not unrequited. On another level, I take it, her love was not in vain because it was valuable, because it generated a value which is still with her, even though, as we know from the title, her lover is dead. And she has not loved "as common Mortals love" (which is presumably another sense in which she has not loved "in vain"). But the poet is not saying that her love was more "spiritual," or even, in the usual sense, more constant than that of "common Mortals." With a brilliant rhythmic modulation we are given two images dramatizing the quality of this love:

  The Fruit of Fire is Ashes,
  The Ocean's tempest dashes
 Wrecks and the dead upon the rocky shore.[8]

In the first stanza we have been told that the Lady's "heroic port /And Beauty" was "Victor even of Time." This is now seen as vigorously ironic. Her beauty does not fade and her "port" remains heroic in spite of all the vicissitudes of time. But the Lady herself, and the love (whose quality is dictated by the Lady's possession of this very beauty and "heroic port"), are peculiarly subject to time. It is this very intensity of love, this "True Passion" (as contrasted with the lukewarm loves of "common Mortals"), that, in its neces-

---

8. Cf. the use of the same image in *Childe Harold*, iii.34. This is all the more striking because of its proximity to the image of the broken mirror (33), which naturally suggests the shattered portrait of the Ode.

sity of exploring the whole range of amorous experience, burns itself out and wrecks the lovers: [9]

> True Passion must the all-searching changes prove,
>> The Agony of Pleasure and of Pain,
>> Till Nothing but the Bitterness remain;
>> And the Heart's Spectre flitting through the brain
> Scoffs at the Exorcism which would remove.

The "Heart's Spectre . . . Scoffs at the Exorcism which would remove [it]" [1] because, among other things, even the ghost of a love such as this is proud and valuable, and because the recognition of this exorcism would imply a recognition of the claims of a rival religion to that of love, one which the lovers have deliberately rejected (see the ends of stanzas one and three).

3

> And where is He thou lovedst? in the tomb,
>> Where should the happy Lover be!
> For him could Time unfold a brighter doom,
>> Or offer aught like thee?
> He in the thickest battle died,
>> Where Death is Pride;

---

9. Cf. *Don Juan,* xiv.94: "Love bears within its breast the very germ / Of Change." See also *The Giaour* (ll. 916–21; my italics):

> To Love the softest hearts are prone,
> But such can ne'er be all his [i.e., Love's] own;
> . . . .
> *And sterner hearts alone may feel*
> *The wound that Time can never heal.*

1. This use of "remove" without an expressed object is, of course, a non-functional ambiguity. There is a partial parallel in the use of "requite" in the "Lines on Hearing that Lady Byron was Ill":

> I am too well avenged!—but 'twas my right;
> Whate'er my sins might be, *thou* wert not sent
> To be the Nemesis who should requite.   [ll. 13–15]

The third stanza opens with two lines of overt irony. The passion of their love has burnt itself out, so there is nothing left for the Lover but to die. That is the "meaning" of the lines. But the full meaning includes the rather extraordinary tonal complexities they suggest. The irony is so strong as to be almost sarcasm—against the "happy Lover" because of his naïveté in supposing that such love as theirs was impervious to time (that is, in being the conventional "happy Lover") and, rather more strongly, against a world in which a great love must end in bitterness and death. Time, over which the Lady's "heroic port /And Beauty" are triumphant (while at the same time it is they, in a sense, that deliver the Lady herself to the tyranny of Time, as experienced by all "true" lovers), once he has done his work, can offer the Lover nothing more than death:

> For him could Time unfold a brighter doom
> Or offer aught like thee?

This is a comment both on the power and the weakness of Time. It is Time that, from one point of view, has put the Lover in his present state; but after such a love there is nothing more in the whole extent of time that the Lover could desire. And so the death that is forced upon him by Time becomes a gesture of his love's triumph over Time. And his death is worthy of his Lady:

> He in the thickest battle died,
> Where Death is Pride.

It is the Lady's pride which has, in a sense, led to the death of their love (and of the Lover), but the manner of his death (as of her living death) is itself proud. The range of meanings implicit in the poet's use of "pride" should by this time be clear.

> And *Thou* his widow—not his bride,
> Wer't not more free—

> *Here* where all love, till Love is made
>   A bondage or a trade,
> *Here*—thou so redolent of Beauty,
> In whom Caprice had seemed a duty,
> *Thou,* who could'st trample and despise
> The holiest chain of human ties
> For him, the dear One in thine eyes,
>   Broke it no more.
> Thy heart was withered to it's Core,
> It's hopes, it's fears, it's feelings o'er:
> Thy Blood grew Ice when *his* was shed,
> And Thou the Vestal of the Dead.

The next lines ("And *Thou* his widow, etc.") present the only apparent difficulty of the poem, i.e. the reference of the presumed "it" of "wer't." But Sir John Murray, who kindly examined the manuscript (in his possession) at my request, confirms my suspicion that what Byron really wrote was "wert." The line, then, would appear to mean that the Lady, who was his widow without having been his bride, was no more free than the Lover from the fatal effects of their love, specifically from the bullet which actually cost him his life (with implied reference to the shattered portrait of the underlying conceit).[2] Here, he says, in our world, love is indeed constant and respectable, but only because it is seen as simply a mechanical bond or a matter of business ("A bondage or a trade").[3] But *"Thou"* (the Lady) hast nothing to do with such a *"Here"* (a fact emphasized by the italics and the emphatic opposition between the words). The Lady is so "redolent of Beauty" that, in her, "Caprice" (a prime quality of the traditional heroine of love poetry, who is also,

2. The punctuation does not seem to encourage this reading, but Byron's pointing is far too erratic to serve as a safe guide. The passage might also read: "But thou, his widow, wert no more free than if thou hadst been bound to him by marriage."

3. Cf. the attitude toward marriage in, especially, the English cantos of *Don Juan.*

of course, by definition "redolent of Beauty") "had seemed
a duty." Her beauty almost demanded she play the role of
the capricious fair; she so looked the part. But this would
have been contrary to her true nature, as we have seen. Had
she been capricious, of course, the tragedy would have been
averted. It is in this way that the poet prepares us to accept
the idea that there is something noble in the very "guilt"
incurred by this love (and notice that he does not gloss over
the fact that it is guilt, or that the ties they have broken are
holy ones). The very fact that she could "trample and de-
spise" (again the note of pride) these holy bonds is presented
as central to what she brought to their love. It is what is cut
off when the Lover is dead. For in spite of the fact that it
was a love that had suffered the vicissitudes of time (it had
"proved" the "all-searching changes" of love), there was a
curious, almost fanatical constancy about it.[4] Their love had
entered its dark night, but it was no less love. When the
Lover dies, the Lady enters a living death. Furthermore, she
becomes a "Vestal of the Dead." She is a virgin priestess
tending a flame of remembrance. But "virgin" only because
her Lover is dead. This is the closest the poet comes to di-
recting any of his irony against the Lady, and it is another
valuable reminder of his own awareness of the realities of
the situation.

4

> Thy Lover died, as All
> Who truly love should die;
> For such are worthy in the fight to fall
> Triumphantly.
> No Cuirass o'er that glowing heart
> The deadly bullet turned apart:

4. There is a delightfully urbane version of this motif in *Beppo* (34),
where we are told that the Count

> . . . was a lover of the good old school,
> Who still become more constant as they cool.

> Love had bestowed a richer Mail,
>   Like Thetis on her Son;
> But hers at last was vain, and thine could fail—
>   The hero's and the lover's race was run.
> Thy worshipped portrait, thy sweet face,
> *Without* that bosom kept it's place
>   As Thou *within*.
> Oh! enviously destined Ball!
> Shivering thine imaged charms and all
>   Those Charms would win:

At the beginning of the fourth stanza the poet turns from the Lady to the Lover. Again it is the Lover's heroic qualities that are emphasized. And again it is the paradox of victory in defeat. "True Passion" leads to death; the Lover has "truly loved"; but in the manner of his death there is triumph. The triumph, however, is presented very curiously. We are told that it was not a cuirass that deflected the bullet from the Lover's heart, as if it had been something connected with the Lady that *had* done so. And, to be sure, the Lover was equipped with "a richer Mail." The comparison with the baptism of Achilles in the River Styx both dignifies the protection given by the portrait (there is a divinity about it) and prepares us for its failure. If it failed, it failed in eminent company. Further, the ball was "enviously *destined*" (my italics). There was something inevitable about the death of the Lover. In a way he "asked for it," just as Achilles knew even when he killed Hector that his own death would follow.[5] Or, stressing the adverb, there is something in the nature of our world that conspires against such loves as this (cf. stanza two).

> Together pierced, the fatal Stroke hath gored
> Votary and Shrine, the adoring and the adored.
>   That Heart's last throb was thine, that blood

5. Achilles is, of course, a classic model of the lover-hero (cf. his "fatal" love of Polyxena).

> Baptized thine Image in it's flood,
> And gushing from the fount of Faith
> O'erflowed with Passion even in Death,
> Constant to thee as in it's hour
> Of rapture in the secret bower.
> Thou too hast kept thy plight full well,
> As many a baffled Heart can tell.

It is pleasant to observe that in this final stanza the poet really does succeed in "drawing the whole poem together." If, he seems to say, the world is governed by a power (Time, Necessity) hostile to lovers, the relation between lover and beloved in itself constitutes a valid form of religion, and one which is never stronger than in its hour of apparent defeat. To make the point quite clear, we are deluged with religious images. The Lover wears the "worshipped" portrait to battle as a kind of holy medal. He is the "Votary" who adores the Lady in her "Shrine." The Lover's blood gives their love a kind of sacramental consecration by baptizing the "Image" of the Lady. His heart is a "fount of *Faith*" (my italics), and his death a kind of "Passion" (the ambiguity is powerful and unmistakable). It must be conceded that the poet's use of the religious imagery is allusive, but it is adequate to its immediate function.[6]

---

6. The motifs of love, religion, and death are brought together in an especially accomplished manner in *The Island*. Speaking of the love of the island maiden Neuha for the Scottish sailor Torquil, we are told of

> . . . Passion's desolating joy.
> Too powerful over every heart, but most
> O'er those who know not how it may be lost;
> O'er those who, burning in the new-born fire,
> Like martyrs revel in their funeral pyre,
> With such devotion to their ecstasy,
> That Life knows no such rapture as to die:
> And die they do.   [II, ll. 112–19]

Notice also the later reference to love as

The conclusion of the poem is managed with great skill. In the first place, the feeling of finality and of controlled emotion is reinforced by the fact that the last eight lines are uninterrupted tetrameter (looking back to the beginning of the poem), all rhymed in couplets. The last four lines, balancing the constancy of the Lady against that of the Lover (two lines each), are set off by the trochaic "Constant." The trochaic variation also emphasizes the quality the last four lines are concerned with. The Lover is as constant in his death far from the Lady as he had been when he was with her on their night of love. And the Lady's constancy is confirmed by the experience of her many unsuccessful suitors.

At this point the poem, which has been concentrating intently on the world of the lovers themselves, opens to include the great world of the society that surrounds them (a note prepared for by the description of the Lady's social charms in the first stanza). But not entirely. The suitors are "baffled." The word is ambiguous. In the first place, they are frustrated, unable to make headway with the Lady. And they are perplexed. They and the world they represent cannot understand such fidelity. Like the love portrayed by Donne in "The Canonization," this love is a mystery to the laity. But "baffled" applies also to the attitude of the speaker. As a man of the world, accustomed to thinking of love in terms of the standards of a highly sophisticated society (dismissing its loftier pretensions with an epigram from La Rochefoucauld, for example), he too is puzzled by the fidelity of the Lady, and the poem is, from one point of view, his own attempt to come to terms with a situation out-

---

     . . . the all-absorbing flame
   Which, kindled by another, grows the same,
   Wrapt in one blaze; the pure, yet funeral pile,
   Where gentle hearts, like Bramins, sit and smile.
               [II, ll. 378–81]

side the range of his previous experience and which cannot be suavely shrugged off. In this context the cynical "motto," suggesting the speaker's usual point of view, becomes a highly refined tribute to the Lady (looked at this way, the most likely Donnean analogue would be "The Relique").[7]

Much of the power of the poem is clearly derived from the complexities inherent in the poet's handling of the terms "love" and "pride." For though this is a poem dealing with a religion of love, the Love the poet presents is at best a very equivocal deity.[8] In the Ode the only love which is not a "Crime" is the mechanical, tradesmen's love of "common Mortals." "True Passion" is frankly criminal. The God Love drives the Lady to madness and sin. And if it is a religion that redeems its votaries from the tyranny of time, it is at the price of first making them peculiarly subject to the vicissitudes of time. But still, love *is* valuable. It is the supreme value of the poem. It is a value, however, that is asserted with a clear awareness of the moral consequences of illicit passion (a subject on which, it might be suggested, a libertine with a strong Calvinist background is singularly well-equipped to pronounce).

Pride, on the other hand, is the traditional enemy to love, and the Lady of the Ode is in the tradition of those proud ladies who wreak such havoc on gentle hearts in song and sonnet. Pride is a mortal sin against the God of Love, and

7. This "turn" or "opening" of the poem at the end is a favorite device of Byron's. He uses it with great skill in his finely reticent "Elegy on the Death of Sir Peter Parker, Bart.," as well as in, for example, "To Romance" and "The Spell Is Broke."

8. Byron's paradoxes sometimes suggest those of Rousseau. Cf. the following comments on love from the "Discourse on the Origin of Inequality": "A tender and pleasant feeling insinuated itself into their souls, and the least opposition turned it into an impetuous fury: with love arose jealousy; discord triumphed, and human blood was sacrificed to the gentlest of all passions" (tr. G. D. H. Cole, *The Social Contract and Discourses*, New York, Dutton, Everyman's Library, 1950, p. 241). But in Byron's view love so "turns" even without "opposition."

nothing is more common than for Love to take his revenge by involving the hardened sinner in a particularly desperate passion. But in the Ode this pride is itself valuable. It is noble. For example, the lines "He in the thickest battle died, / Where Death is Pride" would mean, from one point of view: "Here is what comes of all your pride—the end is only death and ashes (and it serves you both right)." But the emphasis falls rather on the heroism, the nobility of the death. The dichotomy between love and pride introduced in the paradoxes of the first stanza is dissolved as the complexities of each are drawn out and as one is seen as inextricably involved in the other. For only pride could lead to such a love; and such a love is a legitimate source of pride.

Now no one, I fancy, would care to characterize the poem we have been examining as cynical, sentimental, or confused (three of the accusations most commonly brought against Byron). Yet it is centrally Byronic. It exhibits in miniature many of the qualities of *Don Juan,* including the particular kind of paradox characteristic of the longer poem. And any number of parallels, structural, stylistic, and thematic, can be found with other works of Byron (some of which I have tried to suggest in the notes).

Perhaps the most obvious connection between the heroine, at least, of the Ode and *Don Juan* is found in the treatment of Gulbeyaz. Our first introduction to the Lady of the Ode was, it will be recalled, in terms of a paradox. The Lady is both "awful" and "dear," "soft" and "severe." And both modest softness and martial severity would seem to betoken immunity from that passion which they in fact induced. Byron, of course, repeatedly comments on the antithetical nature of Gulbeyaz. Her "large eyes" reveal a "mixture of sensations"—"half voluptuousness and half command" (v.108). Or again, while "Her form had all the *softness* of her sex" (109), "Something *imperial,* or *imperious,* threw / A chain o'er all she did" (110; my italics). Or yet again, we find her rising from the Sultan's bed "pale with conflicts between *Love* and *Pride*" (vi.89; my italics). And the analogy is all the more striking when, remembering that the Lady's "heroic port / And Beauty" had been "Victor even of Time," we learn that Gulbeyaz, whose antithetical qualities have been lovingly rehearsed in the stanzas immediately preceding, is one of those whom "Time to touch forbears / And turns aside his scythe to vulgar things" (v.98).

Byron is fond of this particular antithesis. It appears, for example, not only in the Lady and in Gulbeyaz, but in the object of the two sonnets "To Genevra." In the second sonnet ("Thy cheek is pale with thought") we hear of Genevra's "*majesty* with *sweetness* blending" (my italics), which induces in the lover an attitude of worship, which does not, however, lessen the passionate quality of his attachment to her. While in the first ("Thine eyes' blue tenderness"), he plays once more with the theme of "seeing you thus, who would have thought you thus?" that we have found also in the Ode ("That eye so soft, etc."). The "speaking sadness" of her manner might have made him suppose her "doomed to earthly care," did he not know her "blesséd bosom fraught / With mines of unalloyed and stainless thought." Here again Byron is working with traditional materials. This particular pattern of antitheses had long been used to suggest a peculiar quality of the power of woman. Petrarch, for example, in the sonnet "Una candida cerva," is lured on by Laura's "vista sì dolce superba," [9] while Valmont is fascinated by the combination of "tigress virtue" and "soft sensibility" in the Présidente de Tourvel.[1]

But we have by no means exhausted the use of the an-

---

9. Coleridge (*Poetry, 3,* 70 n. 1) quotes Byron's journal entry of Dec. 18, 1813, to the effect that he "Redde some Italian, and wrote two Sonnets." The second activity seems to be the outcome of the first.

1. *Les Liaisons dangereuses,* p. 245 (Pt. III, Letter 110).

tithesis in *Don Juan*. There is, for example, the "love" and "pride" in Donna Julia's eyes (1.60) or, more significantly, the fact that Zoe, though somewhat older than her mistress, has a "brow less grave" (II.115) than Haidée, of whom we are told that

> . . . in her air
> There was a something which bespoke command,
> As one who was a Lady in the land.　　[116]

For while the primary emphasis is on the "softness" of Haidée (just as, with regard to Gulbeyaz, it is on the "majesty"), we are not to forget the queenly aspect. This comes out particularly in the encounter with Lambro, when she shows herself very much her father's daughter:

> A minute past, and she had been all tears,
> 　　And tenderness, and infancy; but now
> She stood as one who championed human fears—
> 　　Pale, statue-like, and stern, she wooed the blow;
> And tall beyond her sex, and their compeers,
> 　　She drew up to her height, as if to show
> A fairer mark; and with a fixed eye scanned
> Her Father's face—but never stopped his hand.
>
> 　　　　　　　　　　　　　[IV.43]

Not only does her unexpected "championing of human fears" correspond to Juan's later championing of the freedom of the human spirit before the Sultana (v.126–7), but a strong contrast is set up between Haidée and Gulbeyaz. Though both personalities are presented antithetically, and though the terms of the antitheses, as we have seen, are closely analogous, it is the contrast between them that is most striking. Both women, for example, are "queens." Haidée is "Princess of her father's land" (III.72) and Gulbeyaz the favorite wife of a Sultan. But Haidée's regality is largely metaphoric of an important quality of her personality and of the value which "her" episode is designed to embody. (Dudù, while more obviously "A child of Nature," vi.60, could never serve the purpose). Gulbeyaz, on the other hand, is very much the Sultana. One *would*, perhaps, obey both Haidée and Gulbeyaz by virtue of their natural queenliness. But the fact that one *must* obey Gulbeyaz by virtue of her adventitious political position tends to qualify our willingness to do so. As Juan puts it:

> Heads bow, knees bend, eyes watch around a throne,
> And hands obey—our hearts are still our own.
>
> [v.127]

One would be very wrong to think of this as merely political or emotional liberalism; the mistake is perhaps less likely to be made if one recalls the role of freedom in the Ode. It was an essential quality of the Lady that men would freely choose her to reign over them (she ruled "by acclamation"). And it is the *freedom* of the relationship between the Lady and her Lover that sets it off from the vulgar love that is "A bondage or a trade," and that is responsible for the intensity of their devotion (which is, of course, a submission to the bondage of King Love, enthroned in his court in the Lady's heart). An authentic love is necessarily a free love. But, at the same time, a "free love" is at least likely to be a guilty love.

Unlike the Lady of the Ode (or Haidée), Gulbeyaz attempts to compel love. And love, as we have seen, will not respond to force. Furthermore, the love of Gulbeyaz is not far from lust. Juan himself calls it "a Sultana's sensual phantasy" (v.126). And there is nothing very winning in Byron's depiction of the amours of Catherine the Great. The royal harlot is, in fact, a kind of caricature of the antithesis I have been examining: "Her *sweet* smile, and her then *majestic* figure, / Her *plumpness,* her *imperial condescension*" (ix.72; my italics). The marks of tyranny are lust (Gulbeyaz and

Catherine) and sterility (the Castlereagh of the Dedication). That lust and impotence should be equated will not surprise one who has noted the correspondence between "soaring" and "sinking." The Byron of *Don Juan*, we find, is less concerned with "reconciling" opposites than with implying their moral equivalence.

In the first five stanzas of the first canto of his satiric epic, Byron, in a kind of reversal of the Vergilian *ille ego*, elaborately draws our attention to the fact that he is deliberately turning for his organizing principle from war to love, from the warrior to the lover: [2]

> Brave men were living before Agamemnon
>   And since, exceeding valorous and sage,
> A good deal like him too, though quite the same none;
>   But then they shone not on the poet's page,
> And so have been forgotten:—I condemn none,
>   But can't find any in the present age
> Fit for my poem (that is, for my new one);
> So, as I said, I'll take my friend Don Juan.   [1.5]

For Don Juan is, of course, the traditional symbol of the successful lover *par excellence*. And while not morally irreproachable, Byron's Juan is set in strong contrast to the sterility and lust associated with tyranny. For if Juan's virility is manifest, it is equally clear that he is not lustful in the usual sense (which is one of the reasons for his much-discussed "passivity"; Byron's moral forbids a hero who is an active seducer). It is eunuch Castlereaghs and harlot Catherines that lust for power. And if, with Blake (and Byron), one sees war as "a perversion of the sexual impulse," [3] the opposition between lover and warrior, lover

2. Further to call attention to the fact, he concludes the section with two stanzas (6–7) on the differences between *his* epic and those that have gone before.

3. Northrop Frye, *Fearful Symmetry. A Study of William Blake* (Princeton Univ. Press, 1947), p. 262.

and tyrant, becomes clear, as does the close association between lust, sterility, tyranny, and war.

Byron makes his point with almost monotonous insistence. In a bitter parody of the last line of the opening stanza of the *Faerie Queene,* he announces his theme as " 'Fierce loves and faithless wars' " (VII.8).[4] He is quite seriously implying the moral superiority of his epic over that of Spenser. And so we are told of Catherine the Great, the "modern Amazon and Queen of queans" (VI.96), where the military, political, and passionate are neatly brought together. Or again:

> Oh Catherine! (for of all interjections,
> To thee both *oh!* and *ah!* belong, of right,
> In Love and War) how odd are the connections
> Of human thoughts, which jostle in their flight!
> Just now *yours* were cut out in different sections:
> *First* Ismail's capture caught your fancy quite;
> *Next* of new knights, the fresh and glorious batch:
> And *thirdly* he who brought you the despatch!
>
> [IX.65]

But the most interesting of all is the passage describing the door that leads to the "shrine" of the amorous Sultana:

> The giant door was broad, and bright, and high,
> Of gilded bronze, and carved in curious guise;
> Warriors thereon were battling furiously;
> Here stalks the victor, there the vanquished lies;
> There captives led in triumph droop the eye,
> And in perspective many a squadron flies.   [V.86]

The diction of the passage, vaguely early *Childe Harold,* strikes one as an attempt to suggest the tradition of romance epic, with its matter of loves and battles (*Childe Harold* is, of course, a "romaunt"). The impression is heightened when one observes that the whole passage is distinctly reminiscent

4. Fierce warres and faithful loves shall moralize my song (*Faerie Queene*).

of the brazen door and adjoining battle scenes of Dido's temple (*Aeneid,* Bk. I, ll. 445 ff.), with its associations of passion and violent death. And when one adds the curious appropriateness of the fact that the door to the room of the royal seductress should be opened by muscular but misshapen pigmies (87–90), one has an associative pattern of some resonance.

Furthermore, quite apart from the natural connection of war and lust with tyranny, love itself is seen as inextricably involved in violence. To the poet of the Ode it is apparently axiomatic that the Lover *would* go to war. We simply find him there, with no explanations felt necessary. The first three affairs of Don Juan end in violence and the fourth is prefaced by it. So that while it is necessary to be aware of the contrast between the warrior as hero and the lover as hero, it is equally necessary, because of the paradoxical nature of love itself, to see the lover as warrior. This opportunity is provided by the Siege of Ismail.

I have already commented on the fact that the attitude adopted toward the Siege of Ismail is, for Byron, singularly uncompromising. It is well known that Byron officially deplored wars of aggression, while defending and even exalting those fought in defense of one's country (cf. *Don Juan* VII.40). But he was often prepared to appreciate the pathos and splendor of battle even in a cause for which he was not an unqualified partisan (the fine Waterloo stanzas in *Childe Harold,* III, are a case in point). Byron's treatment of the Siege of Ismail is, however, remarkably stern, the only major exception being the rather tasteless humor about "Wherefore the ravishing did not begin" (VIII.132) which Byron had left over from "The Devil's Drive," where it was in place.[5]

5. The passage can be defended thematically as part of the war-lust motif. The same theme comes out with some brilliance in the poet's allusion to the "Captain bold, in Halifax" (VII.19), and again in the stanzas on Semiramis (II.155–6).

But to observe that in this case the poet does not choose to emphasize the more glamorous aspects of battle is not to say that the treatment is simple. The Siege of Ismail is a prime manifestation of that "waste and icy clime" over which the poet is to play the northern lights of his art. There are, for example, the two admirable elegiac stanzas with which Canto VII concludes, or the tribute to the stoical old Pacha, or the death of the Khan and his five sons. And for all his hatred of aggressive war, some of Byron's finest passages deal with the attacking Russians. For example:

> They fell as thick as harvests beneath hail,
>   Grass before scythes, or corn below the sickle,
> Proving that trite old truth, that Life's as frail
>   As any other boon for which men stickle.
> The Turkish batteries thrashed them like a flail,
>   Or a good boxer, into a sad pickle
> Putting the very bravest, who were knocked
> Upon the head before their guns were cocked.

> [VIII.43]

One of the triumphs of Byron's art (and his humanity) is his depiction of the Russians as poor devils caught in a nasty situation, savage because men in such circumstances are apt to be so. This lack of personal animus makes it possible for the poet to lament their fall, as he does in the curious stanza quoted above. The first line by itself could easily be taken "straight." There is nothing overtly humorous about it. But the two variants on the introductory simile provided by the second line make us feel less secure. There is suddenly something unnerving about this cold-blooded toying with images of violent death. We cannot react as we could, say, to a developed Homeric simile using the same tenor and vehicle. This feeling is only increased by the offhand cynicism of lines 3–4 and the flippant versions of the simile in 5–6 ("like a flail, / Or a good boxer"). But at the same time we are aware of something else, of pity for them simply as men taking a beating, a pity controlled but not negated by the passages of superficial cynicism.[6]

But when all this has been granted, it must be admitted that the Siege of Ismail is on the whole strikingly simple and straightforward. The reason for that may be that Byron is anxious not to obscure the real horror of what his hero is doing. A more glamorous treatment, even the tone taken toward the battles of Talavera and Waterloo in *Childe Harold*, would have made Juan's actions more understandable. We might even sympathize. But it is remarkable that Byron comes closer to being directly critical of Juan in the battle cantos than anywhere else in the poem with the exception of the following and thematically closely related episode at the Russian court.

As we would expect, Juan acquits himself creditably in his first experience with battle. He shows himself both gallant and humane (or as humane as is possible under the circumstances). He saves the child Leila and he joins with Johnson in trying to induce the brave old Khan to give them an excuse to save him—and then joins in killing him when he proves obdurate. But Juan's sentimental farewell to the Turkish women concludes with the sardonic:

> While their belovéd friends began to arm,
> To burn a town which never did them harm.
>
> [vii.76]

And even while praising his "broth of a boy" for his unthinking good nature, the poet hints at certain limitations of this kind of amiability:

> But Juan was quite "a broth of a boy,"
> A thing of impulse and a child of song;

6. Byron's finest achievement of this sort is the splendid Koutousow section of Canto viii (70–6), which he juxtaposes to the idyllic lines on Daniel Boone (61–7).

Now swimming in the sentiment of joy,
　　Or the *sensation* (if that phrase seem wrong),
And afterward, if he must needs destroy,
　　In such good company as always throng
To battles, sieges, and that kind of pleasure,
No less delighted to employ his leisure;

But always without malice: if he warred
　　Or loved, it was with what we call "the best
Intentions," which form all Mankind's *trump card,*
　　To be produced when brought up to the test.
The statesman—hero—harlot—lawyer—ward
　　Off each attack, when people are in quest
Of their designs, by saying they *meant well;*
'Tis pity "that such meaning should pave Hell."

[VIII.24–5]

"Natural man," as one would expect, is no more dependable
than "human nature" itself (VIII.82). Still more damaging,
however, is a passage at the end of Canto VIII, where the poet
is summing up with regard to the siege:

If here and there some transient trait of pity
　　Was shown, and some more noble heart broke through
Its bloody bond, and saved, perhaps, some pretty
　　Child, or an agéd, helpless man or two—
What's this in one annihilated city,
　　Where thousand loves, and ties, and duties grew?

[124]

Here the poet shows himself far from sentimental about his
hero's generous impulses. It is hard not to associate the
"transient trait of pity" with, say, the blood of Juan "cur-
dling" at "some heavy groan" (55), the saving of the "pretty
child" with the rescue of Leila, and that of the "agéd helpless man" with the attempt to spare the life of the old (but
by no means helpless) Khan.

　　At the very end of the battle cantos, as the poet is sending his hero off to Petersburg and Catherine, he tells us what it is that makes men fight, what human passion is behind wars. It is simply "vanity" (140), the self-love that was so conspicuous a quality in Donna Inez (1.20) and Wellington (ix.5), and is so lacking in Dudù (vi.54). It is self-love that makes men want to believe women's lies (vi.19) and which is behind the self-deception of Donna Julia (1.77–81, 106). And finally it was self-love that caused Juan, after his noble speeches to Gulbeyaz, to become the official favorite of Catherine the Great (ix.68–72). But in the world of *Don Juan* love itself is under the same stigma:

> Love is vanity,
> Selfish in its beginning as its end.[7]   [ix.73]

Love, which should be a means of overcoming self, of living in and for another person, is itself essentially egoistic. The remedy merely aggravates the disorder. It is the same paradox which, in other terms, we have met so often before.

For Byron is very conscientious about putting love in its place, reminding us that it is only one passion among others. It is listed indifferently with Glory, the Grape, and Gold as objects of human hope (ii.179), with Glory, Power, and Treasure as possible human ends (1.133), and with "long travel, Ennui, [and] Slaughter" as indulgences that call for a "pick-me-up" (ii.180). Or, to place it chronologically, it is simply the "first net which spreads its deadly mesh" for men, only to be followed by "Ambition, Avarice, Vengeance, Glory" in our later years (v.22). Or again:

> Love or lust makes Man sick, and wine much sicker;
> Ambition rends, and gaming gains a loss.   [xii.4]

In a very important passage at the end of Canto ii (214–15) Byron supplies us with two conceits dramatizing

---

7. Byron is quite possibly thinking of the passage from Buffon's *Histoire naturelle* that he quotes in one of the notes to the second letter in the Bowles Controversy (*LJ*, 5, 572).

the analogy between a fallen nature given over to disorder and mutability and a fallen human nature similarly condemned. I have commented on the first of these ("The heart is like the sky, etc.") in the preceding chapter. It is the second octave with which we are immediately concerned:

> The liver is the lazaret of bile,
>> But very rarely executes its function,
> For the first passion stays there such a while,
>> That all the rest creep in and form a junction,
> Like knots of vipers on a dunghill's soil—
>> Rage, fear, hate, jealousy, revenge, compunction—
> So that all mischiefs spring up from this entrail,
> Like Earthquakes from the hidden fire called "central."
>
> [II.215]

It is this "first passion" (clearly love) that opens the way for the other passions ("Rage, fear, hate, jealousy, revenge, compunction") and to all the subsequent evils of life ("all mischiefs"). The point is worth pausing over, because it seems to me that this is to be taken rather seriously. In other words, when Byron insists that "the moral of this composition" is that (VI.87)

> The Nightingale that sings with the deep thorn,
>> Which fable places in her breast of wail,
> Is lighter far of heart and voice than those
> Whose headlong passions form their proper woes,

I am inclined to take his word for it. As we have seen, there is much more to it than the poet suggests here. But within certain limits the generalization seems a fair one. In the passage just quoted he is referring specifically to Gulbeyaz, but one is clearly intended to think also of the passion of Donna Julia, the jealousy of Alfonso, the rage of Lambro and Haidée (IV.45), the "lust of Power" (VII.40) of Potemkin and Catherine, and so on.

Byron has been careful in the first canto to give us a case history of the effect of passion on the human personality. For the story of Donna Julia, with all its light-heartedness, is a careful study in moral and personal degeneration resulting from acquiescence in passion. What Steffan has seen as merely another example of Byron's inconsistency or expediency is really a particularly fine example of his honesty and precision, both artistic and moral.[8]

Byron gives us a careful and detailed account of the process by which Julia maneuvers herself into a fatal intimacy with Juan. Being older than Juan and a married woman, she is much more conscious of what is involved than he can be. She is responsible, but she is not blamed. Not only are there extenuating circumstances (the age of Alfonso and the plots of Inez), but she does try to overcome her love. Her heart

> . . . had deeper thoughts in store
> She must not own, but cherished more the while
> For that compression in its burning core.   [1.72]

The very fact that she made an effort to suppress her love only contributes to the violence of the final explosion. It is almost like a physical law, as if love were a kind of steam. Byron's attitude toward restraint is ambiguous, but at this point in the poem he is clearly thinking of it largely in quantitative terms—in terms of the force of the final outburst. Only later, when he comes to the English cantos and Lady Adeline, will restraint be valued for the qualitative improvement it makes possible in both personality and passion.[9]

There is no need to rehearse the carefully developed progress of Julia's self-deception. She falls, of course, and the affair has been under way for some time when we meet her

8. *Variorum, 1,* 188–9.
9. See below, p. 118 n. 1.

next, in the bedroom scene. Here the moral effects of illicit
love are made brutally apparent. From a gentle, warm-
hearted, impulsive girl who has to go to considerable trou-
ble in contriving to deceive herself as to her real motives
and desires, she has become an accomplished schemer and
deceiver. This is seen in the brilliantly improvised attack
she delivers against Alfonso. She is hard, worldly, and dishonest. Her situation is beautifully dramatized in a final
descriptive stanza, the point of which Steffan has misunder-
stood:

> She ceased, and turned upon her pillow; pale
>   She lay, her dark eyes flashing through their tears,
> Like skies that rain and lighten; as a veil
>   Waved and o'ershading her wan cheek, appears
> Her streaming hair; the black curls strive, but fail
>   To hide the glossy shoulder, which uprears
> Its snow through all;—her soft lips lie apart,
> And louder than her breathing beats her heart.

[1.158]

Steffan suggests that this is an unsuccessful attempt to
achieve a "sensuous, pathetic effect" in "the lush manner of
Keats." [1] And if that were what Byron sought here he certainly failed most dismally. But it should be clear that nothing of the sort is intended. Indeed, such an effect at this
point would be dishonest both aesthetically and morally.
Steffan is reacting to something that is really in the stanza,
but he is not accurately analyzing his reaction. The stanza
is theatrical, and deliberately so. It is part of the measure of
degeneration from the rather innocent Julia we had met before. She is a woman in a dangerous situation lying to her
husband. She is afraid and she is acting. The false pathos of
the passage is the pathos deliberately created by Julia in her
attempt to sway Alfonso. And it is no accident that she
strikes a pose calculated delicately to reveal her charms. The

1. *Variorum, 1,* 341-2.

passage is showy, overheated, overdone, because that is the quality of the gesture it is designed to dramatize. There is an almost hysterical quality about it. Julia is terrified— "And louder than her breathing beats her heart." This much at least is genuine.

The third stage in the decline and fall of Donna Julia is represented by the letter. Steffan is helpful here. Commenting on the stanza devoted to the physical appearance of the letter, he asks: "Is there not at the end some penetrating laughter at the delicate postures of sentiment in the little ironies about the 'gilt-edged paper' and 'neat little crow-quill,' her sunflower seal of 'superfine' vermillion wax, with its motto 'cut upon a white cornelian'—'*Elle vous suit partout*'?" [2] He is, of course, perfectly right in seeing irony here. It is not savage irony, to be sure. The tone is one of quiet, almost tender mockery. But Julia is not permitted to be merely pathetic. The rather indulgent self-pity of the letter itself and the elegance of its appearance suggest that Julia is well aware of the dramatic possibilities of her situation and is determined to play the part to the hilt. One hardly blames her very much, but one is not taken in. The distance from the Julia we used to know is obvious. And we are never allowed to forget that she brought herself to this state by her love for Juan.

But it is through the pure love of Haidée that Byron chooses to make his point most unambiguously clear:

> Oh, Love! thou art the very God of evil,
> For, after all, we cannot call thee Devil.
>
> [II.205]

Or, even more potently, we are told that in the early days of her love for Juan Haidée was

> . . . too deeply blest
> To feel the poison through her spirit creeping,

2. *Ibid.,* p. 280.

> Or know who rested there, a foe to rest,
> Had soiled the current of her sinless years,
> And turned her pure heart's purest blood to tears!
>
> [III.1]

There is something "in this world of ours / Which makes it fatal to be loved" (III.2)—words that call to mind the "Ode to a Lady" (the epigraph to which appears in a couplet three octaves later). "Evil," "poison," "fatal" are, as Elizabeth Boyd has pointed out, strong words to use of the Haidée idyll.[3] But Byron is relentless. Even the elegiac lines on Haidée's death (themselves highly reminiscent of the Ode) have to bear a heavy moral weight: [4]

> Valour was his, and Beauty dwelt with her:
> If she loved rashly, her life paid for wrong—
> A heavy price must all pay who thus err,
> In some shape; let none think to fly the danger.
> For soon or late Love is his own avenger.   [IV.73]

Even Haidée, "Nature's child," is not exempt from the inexorable laws under which "this world of ours" operates. "In her first passion," says the poet, "Woman loves her lover, / In all the others all she loves is Love" (III.3). And presumably this applies also to Haidée. Her love retains its purity only by her death.

It is worth noticing that this complication of the love

---

3. *Byron's Don Juan,* pp. 61–2.
4. Cf. also II.192:

> Alas! they were so young, so beautiful,
>   So lonely, loving, helpless, and the hour
> Was that in which the Heart is always full,
>   And, having o'er itself no further power,
> Prompts deeds Eternity can not annul,
>   But pays off moments in an endless shower
> Of hell-fire—all prepared for people giving
> Pleasure or pain to one another living.

idyll was not an afterthought. It is implicit in the lines of description that first introduce us (and Juan) to Haidée:

> Her hair, I said, was auburn; but her eyes
>   Were black as Death, their lashes the same hue,
> Of downcast length, in whose silk shadows lies
>   Deepest attraction; for when to the view
> Forth from its raven fringe the full glance flies,
>   Ne'er with such force the swiftest arrow flew;
> 'Tis as the snake late coiled, who pours his length
> And hurls at once his venom and his strength.
>
> [II.117]

One should notice especially the way Byron exploits the possibilities for ambiguity in the blackness of Haidée's eyes. Black is the color of beauty and fascination ("Deepest attraction"), but also of mystery, danger, or even evil ("Death," the "arrow," the "snake").[5] Here again the motifs of poison ("venom") and of violence (the "strength" hurled when the serpent strikes). Here again there is charm and beauty concealing violence and death. Or rather, here again we see how charm and beauty are inextricably involved in violence and death.

Reference to the serpent, with its inevitable satanic associations, helps prepare us for another allusion of still greater complexity, this time with reference to Gulbeyaz:

> And yet a headlong, headstrong, downright She,
>   Young, beautiful, and daring—who would risk
> A throne—the world—the universe—to be
>   Beloved in her own way—and rather whisk
> The stars from out the sky, than not be free
>   As are the billows when the breeze is brisk—

---

5. Byron's development of the ambiguity of the color black is strikingly analogous to Sidney's treatment (also in terms of eyes) in *Astrophel and Stella*, xx ("Fly, fly, my friends!").

Though such a She's a devil (if there be one),
Yet she would make full many a Manichaean.

[VI.3]

The allusion is to Rev. 12:3–4, where the "great red dragon" draws down "the third part of the stars of heaven" with his tail (hence "whisk"). Byron makes the traditional association between the dragon and the Devil (cf. *Paradise Lost,* Bk. II, ll. 689–92). Even as Satan was willing to take the risk of eternal punishment in order to be free of God's dominion, so a "headlong, headstrong, downright She" is willing to take comparable risks and suffer comparable punishment in order to exercise her passion in freedom.[6] And while such a woman provides as close an approximation to the satanic as one might wish, there is a charm about her which induces us to give the devil his due. One thinks of the earlier lines on Gulbeyaz:

Her form had all the softness of her sex,
    Her features all the sweetness of the Devil,
When he put on the Cherub to perplex
    Eve, and paved (God knows how) the road to evil.

[V.109]

As Willis Pratt points out in a note to this passage,[7] there was an iconographical tradition which depicted the Devil tempting Eve as a beautiful, angelic figure ending in the scaly coils of a serpent. The whole pattern of association is strongly suggestive of the "Ode to a Lady." Beauty and

---

6. Cf. *Don Juan,* XII.64, where we are told that "Eve's was a trifling case" compared to that of an English married woman who "makes or takes love in downright earnest."

7. *Variorum, 4,* 133 (cf. *Poetry, 6,* 249 n. 1). Byron is probably thinking of the "Epistle to Dr. Arbuthnot" (ll. 330–1):

Eve's Tempter thus the Rabbins have exprest,
A Cherub's face, a Reptile all the rest.

But see also the reference to "that dread yet lovely serpent" in the lines on the Fall in *The Bride of Abydos* (I, l. 159).

love are recognized as in some sense evil and at the same time uniquely valuable.

For if Don José's infidelity to Donna Inez was the consequence of his being "a lineal son of Eve" (1.18), his son's equally illicit love for Haidée is seen as a kind of restoration of the paradisal state lost by our First Parents. "First love," we are told, is "all / Which Eve has left her daughters since her fall" (11.189). To Juan and Haidée, "Each was an angel, and earth Paradise" (11.204). For them to be together was "another Eden" (IV.10). The two of them create in their love the state of bliss from which not only man but each man in his own life has fallen. Insofar as man has known Paradise, the poet suggests, this was its nature.

And the issue is in every case the same—a fall. As both the Miltonic analogy and Byron's paradoxical world view should lead us to expect, there is a serpent in this Garden. Or rather, there are three serpents. Taking them in reverse order, there is first of all the arms of Lambro that tear Haidée away from Juan:

> His arms were like a serpent's coil: then flew
>> Upon their prey, as darts an angry asp,
> The file of pirates.   [IV.48]

The appropriateness of Lambro as a force disruptive of the island paradise, a serpent in the Eden of Juan and Haidée, is clear enough. First of all, he is an adult, and a father. As such, he is well adapted to suggest the force of the past and the adult world pressing down relentlessly on this frail Eden. The notable lack of hostility toward Lambro is explained by the fact that Byron is simply assuming that of course he *would* act as he does. He acts almost impersonally, as a kind of allegorical function. And the force of it is heightened when one recalls that to Byron piracy is metaphoric of the essential nature of the activities of men of the "great world" (111.14).

Furthermore, the suitability of Lambro for the role he

plays with regard to Juan and Haidée is related to the circumstances of his own life. For Lambro is a good deal more than a semicomic version of the Byronic hero. We have already seen something of the thematic importance of his elaborately antithetical personality. And surely it is not irrelevant that the poet so insists on the innocence and good nature of the essential Lambro which has been distorted and perverted by his experience of the world:

> Quick to perceive, and strong to bear, and meant
>   For something better, if not wholly good;
> His Country's wrongs and his despair to save her
> Had stung him from a slave to an enslaver.
>
> The love of power, and rapid gain of gold,
>   The hardness by long habitude produced,
> The dangerous life in which he had grown old,
>   The mercy he had granted oft abused,
> The sights he was accustomed to behold,
>   The wild seas, and wild men with whom he cruised,
> Had cost his enemies a long repentance,
> And made him a good friend, but bad acquaintance.
>
> [III.53–4]

The fact that Lambro himself so pre-eminently embodies this very process of succumbing to experience further increases the symbolic range of the role he plays with regard to the lovers. He is, in a sense, a personification of experience.

If Lambro and his crew are the first serpent, the second is rather more abstract:

> They [the lovers] were all summer; lightning might assail
>   And shiver them to ashes, but to trail
> *A long and snake-like life of dull decay*
>   Was not for them—they had too little clay.
>
> [IV.9; my italics]

From this serpent Haidée, at least, was spared, except insofar as the melancholy circumstances of her death were the simple consequence of the extension of her love in time. For time, in a fallen world of mutability, is as ruthless a foe of what we have been calling "innocence" as any external social force can ever be. It is life that is, from this point of view, the real enemy. Life itself, as Frost might say, "is enough, and would suffice."

On the third serpent I have commented already, with regard to the stanza on Haidée's eyes:

> 'Tis as the snake late coiled, who pours his length,
> And hurls at once his venom and his strength.
>
> [II.117]

Here we see that the most potent enemy to innocence (as embodied in young love) is simply love itself. The most powerful force undermining the paradisal relationship is the very force that made it a paradise in the first place.

The crucial passage occurs at the end of the section in which the poet lists the "sweetnesses" of life:

> But sweeter still than this, than these, than all,
>   Is first and passionate Love—it stands alone,
> Like Adam's recollection of his fall;
>   The Tree of Knowledge has been plucked—all's known—
> And Life yields nothing further to recall
>   Worthy of this ambrosial sin, so shown,
> No doubt in fable, as the unforgiven
> Fire which Prometheus filched for us from Heaven.
>
> [I.127]

This should be compared with the following:

> Oh thou *"teterrima causa"* of all *"belli"*—
>   Thou gate of Life and Death—thou nondescript!
> Whence is our exit and our entrance,—well I

May pause in pondering how all souls are dipped
In thy perennial fountain:—how man *fell* I
   Know not, since Knowledge saw her branches
          stripped
Of her first fruit; but how he *falls* and rises
   Since,—*thou* hast settled beyond all surmises.   [IX.55]

The second passage is especially striking if we recall what
has been suggested above about the relation between love
and war, and how the poet evidently wants us to feel about
it. Here he is ironically glorying in the fact that war (a
prime expression of the fallen state of man) is the consequence of the passion of love, which has within itself the
capacity to repair the damage it does. It is through love,
to reverse the emphasis of Byron's line, that man "falls and
rises." But this is only a more complexly ironic version of
what the first passage puts more explicitly. "First and passionate love" is "Like Adam's recollection of his fall." Such
a love recreates for the individual son of Adam the paradisal
state lost by the first Adam through his experience of such
a love. But, if the sin be "ambrosial," no attempt is made
to deny that it is a sin. One is reminded yet again of the
Ode. Love is the fire Prometheus brought down to man
from heaven. But there is something wrong about the gift.
It is "unforgiven." Furthermore, and Byron altered the
first version to bring this out,[8] it is stolen—"filched." It is
not rightfully ours.

Byron's Prometheanism is not always understood. Wilson
Knight, who comes closer than most to seeing what Byron is
up to, writes: "Highest virtue is, and must be, anti-social;
more, it *plays with fire,* like Prometheus, and is therefore
as near the Satanic as the Divine. The Divine, as it were,
becomes Satanic under opposition, and may begin to endure
the *fiery* guilt of the great 'scorpion' passage in *The*

---

8. *Variorum,* 2, 90.

Giaour." [9] All of which seems to underestimate substantially the element of aberration or guilt in the possession of the fire itself. The issue is less that of the Divine's becoming Satanic under opposition than the much more orthodox sin of a being of a lower order's appropriating gifts and privileges not his according to the nature of things. It has as much in common with religious as with Romantic Prometheanism.

Since the point is of some importance, it may be well to glance at the poem in which Byron has dealt most exhaustively with the Prometheus theme, *Childe Harold* III and IV. In his section on the Apollo Belvidere Byron writes:

And if it be Prometheus stole from Heaven
  The fire which we endure—it was repaid
  By him to whom the energy was given
  Which this poetic marble hath arrayed
  With an eternal Glory—which, if made
  By human hands, is not of human thought—
  And Time himself hath hallowed it, nor laid
  One ringlet in the dust—nor hath it caught
A tinge of years, but breathes the flame with which 'twas
    wrought. [IV.163]

Notice that the fire which Prometheus gave to man is regarded in a highly ambivalent fashion. It is "The fire which we *endure*," and, at the same time, it is "from Heaven." Further, there is a definite suggestion of guilt in the allusion to the Prometheus myth. The fire is "stolen" (cf. the "filched" fire of *Don Juan*), and we suffer as a result of the theft. At the same time, it is through art, made possible by the crime that made it necessary, that the inadequacies of a fallen state are overcome. Man transcends mutability

9. G. Wilson Knight, *Lord Byron. Christian Virtues* (New York, Oxford Univ. Press, 1953), pp. 247–8. Knight's discussion of the Prometheanism of, especially, *Child Harold*, is valuable.

("Time himself hath hallowed" the statue) in a work of art that serves as expiation for a sin whose consequences alone make such expiation possible. This circular argument constitutes, as we have seen, a central Byronic paradox: the only means of coping with the fact of fall are themselves inextricably involved in the peril of fall. For it is a peculiarity of Byron's Prometheanism that he is a by no means uncritical partisan of the Thief of Fire.

Chapter 4

"MY POEM'S EPIC"

WHILE BYRON'S READING of the myth of the Fall is one of the most important means of organizing the materials of *Don Juan,* it is not the only one. In the first chapter of this study I attempted an analysis of the Dedication in terms of the poet's evident awareness of the traditional concepts of genre and stylistic level. The second and third chapters emphasized certain points at which stylistic metaphor fused with the metaphor of the Fall, particularly in the imagery of flight or soaring. It was further suggested that while the poet is conscious of moral danger in flight (it leads to a fall like that of Lucifer), some sort of flight is essential to the poetic vocation (Wordsworth sticks to the ground and is savagely attacked for it). It is with this paradox (and the paradoxical world view of which it is a manifestation) that the poet's version of the myth of the Fall is designed to deal.

Now by "soaring" Byron refers to that heroic tradition of which the epic was the supreme expression. "A heroic poem, truly such, is undoubtedly the greatest work which the soul of man is capable to perform." Dryden had said that at the beginning of the Dedication of his translation of Vergil,[1] and Byron had been brought up in that tradition.

1. *Essays of John Dryden,* ed. W. P. Ker (2 vols. Oxford, Clarendon Press, 1900), 2, 154. Cf. the note to *English Bards,* l. 225:

So it might be well to consider a bit more seriously than is usual Byron's observations on the epic form and the claims he makes for *Don Juan* as an epic. The question, be it understood, is not whether *Don Juan* is or is not an epic, and in what sense. That is not a very interesting question. Just as it is the metaphoric possibilities of the myth of the Fall that interest us, it is the metaphoric implications of the concept of epic with which we are primarily concerned. As was the case with the myth, Byron's interpretation of this traditional material is highly individual; but for our generation, at least, it is the awareness of tradition which must be emphasized.

Byron is very emphatic, both in prose and verse, as to the epic pretensions of *Don Juan*. To confine ourselves to the poem itself, he contrasts himself with "Most epic poets," who "plunge *'in medias res'* " (1.6). Or, more simply, he announces "My poem's epic," and submits a highly orthodox prospectus:

> My poem's epic, and is meant to be
>   Divided in twelve books; each book containing,
> With Love and War, a heavy gale at sea,
>   A list of ships, and captains, and king's reigning,
> New characters; the episodes are three:
>   A panoramic view of Hell's in training,
> After the style of Virgil and of Homer,
> So that my name of Epic's no misnomer.   [1.200]

And then from time to time we have passing references to "this Epic" (xvi.3), or, with more precision, to "this Epic

---

We beg Mr. Southey's pardon: "Madoc disdains the degraded title of Epic." See his Preface. Why is Epic degraded? and by whom? Certainly the late Romaunts of Masters Cottle, Laureat Pye, Ogilvy, Hole, and gentle Mistress Cowley, have not exalted the Epic Muse; but, as Mr. Southey's poem "disdains the appellation," allow us to ask—has he substituted anything better in its stead? or must he be content to rival Sir Richard Blackmore in the quantity as well as quality of his verse?

Satire" (xiv.99). The question here, I suppose, is whether
the epic tradition and the fun Byron has with it have any
special bearing on the meaning of *Don Juan,* or whether the
humor is incidental.

The passage quoted above is surely largely playful. But
there are one or two things that deserve comment. There is,
for example, the bland pairing of "Love and War" as things
which naturally go together and which appear together in
epic (primarily, of course, the *Iliad*). I have made some suggestions in the preceding chapter as to the implications of
Byron's initial turning from the warrior to the lover for
the hero of his poem. For when we read "I want a hero" we
are clearly intended to hear in the background "I sing of
arms and the man." Furthermore, Byron's uncertainty as to
his hero is not merely a comment on the nineteenth century's presumed inability to supply an acceptable equivalent
to Achilles or Aeneas. The whole concept of the warrior-
hero is, as we have seen, vigorously called in question. Again
and again Byron associates war with the epic and suggests
that the traditional heroic poem compromises itself morally
by its apparent glorification of bloodshed. In addition to
the parody of Spenser cited above, one thinks particularly
of the bitter reference to "conquest and its consequences,
which / Make Epic poesy so rare and rich" (viii.90), or his
comment on the savagery of the Cossacks, that "Achilles'
self was not more grim and gory" (vii.14). Or there is the
brilliant stanza of Canto viii where his invocation of the
Muse (particularly common in the course of epic battles)
takes the form of a curse:

> Oh, blood and thunder! and oh, blood and wounds!
>   These are but vulgar oaths, as you may deem,
> Too gentle reader! and most shocking sounds:—
>   And so they are; yet thus is Glory's dream
> Unriddled, and as my true Muse expounds

At present such things, since they are her theme,
So be they her inspirers! Call them Mars,
Bellona, what you will—they mean but wars.   [VIII.1]

It does not, then, seem reckless to suggest that, in his lesser way and from his essentially secular and predominantly rationalist point of view, Byron is attempting as radical a redefinition of the nature of epic and the epic hero as was Milton in *Paradise Lost.*

There is at least one other striking similarity between the epic poems of Milton and Byron: both deal with a loss of innocence. And in both cases the attitude toward this loss is distinctly equivocal. Byron's tone in *Don Juan* had been set many years before in a poem called "To Romance," which appeared in *Hours of Idleness* in 1807. "To Romance" is not a great lyric by any means, but it is interesting in that it suggests attitudes characteristic of the later Byron. It begins:

> Parent of golden dreams, Romance!
>   Auspicious Queen of childish joys,
> Who lead'st along, in airy dance,
>   Thy votive train of girls and boys;
> At length, in spells no longer bound,
>   I break the fetters of my youth;
> No more I tread thy mystic round,
>   But leave thy realms for those of Truth.

The poet's attitude toward Romance seems at first wholly sympathetic. She is "Parent of golden dreams" and "Auspicious Queen of childish joys." The first note of qualification is suggested by the adjective "childish"—which may, to be sure, mean no more than "youthful"—and by the insubstantiality of "airy." The second adjective is especially well chosen, suggesting as it does the charm and the weakness of Romance. Then we learn that the "votive train of girls and boys" takes part in the "airy dance" only because it is under a "spell." The "airy dance" and "mystic round" send the unwitting young people pointlessly around and around in a circle getting nowhere, which action is seen imaginatively as forming a fetter. But the poet claims to have broken out of the charmed circle (or chain) and left the realms of Romance for those of Truth. The whole is quite evidently a variant on the lines of Pope we have had occasion to glance at above:

> That not in Fancy's Maze he wander'd long,
> But stoop'd to Truth, and moraliz'd his song.
> ["Epistle to Dr. Arbuthnot," ll. 340–1]

There is the same opposition between Fancy (l. 13 in Byron's poem) and Truth. The "Maze" corresponds to the "mystic round" and the "stooping to Truth" (the motion of a falcon toward its lure) with the renunciation of "soaring" on "fancied pinions" ("To Romance," l. 28). One sees here an early form of some of the notions and images we have been tracing both in the Dedication and in *Don Juan* itself.

Now one of the most striking characteristics of the *persona* is that he is no longer the man he once was. This is a source of mingled satisfaction and regret:

> "*Non ego hoc ferrem calidus juventâ*
>   *Consule Planco,*" Horace said, and so
> Say I; by which quotation there is meant a
>   Hint that some six or seven good years ago
> (Long ere I dreamt of dating from the Brenta)
>   I was most ready to return a blow,
> And would not brook at all this sort of thing
> In my hot youth—when George the Third was King.
>
> But now at thirty years my hair is grey—
>   (I wonder what it will be like at forty?
> I thought of a peruke the other day—)

My heart is not much greener; and, in short, I
Have squandered my whole summer while 'twas May,
  And feel no more the spirit to retort; I
Have spent my life, both interest and principal,
And deem not, what I deemed—my soul invincible.

No more—no more—Oh! never more on me
  The freshness of the heart can fall like dew,
Which out of all the lovely things we see
  Extracts emotions beautiful and new,
Hived in our bosoms like the bag o' the bee.
  Think'st thou the honey with those objects grew?
Alas! 'twas not in them, but in thy power
To double even the sweetness of a flower.

No more—no more—Oh! never more, my heart,
  Canst thou be my sole world, my universe!
Once all in all, but now a thing apart,
  Thou canst not be my blessing or my curse:
The illusion's gone for ever, and thou art
  Insensible, I trust, but none the worse,
And in thy stead I've got a deal of judgment,
Though Heaven knows how it ever found a lodgment.

                                        [1.212–15]

The first two stanzas express a mellow, half-amused con-
sciousness of change and loss. In the last two the tone is that
of the romantic *cri*—one of Byron's finest efforts in a mode
by no means easy to bring off. The trick rhymes of the first
two are dropped in the second, to be picked up again in the
final "judgment/lodgment" rhyme, as the tone once more
begins to lighten.

The theme of the concluding stanzas is the essential sub-
jectivity of human value. It is Coleridge saying (in "Dejec-
tion"):

        O Lady! we receive but what we give,
        And in our life alone does Nature live.

Or Madame de Merteuil: "This charm we think we find in others exists in us, and love alone embellishes so much the beloved person." [2] The theist Coleridge is lamenting a fall from grace (he, unlike the Lady, whose imaginative vision is unimpaired, is no longer "guided from above"), so that the fallen world of "Reality's dark dream" exists for him simply as fallen. It is no longer molded and illuminated by the sacramental power of imagination. While this is not too far from what Byron is suggesting in the "Aurora Borealis" passage discussed in Chapter 2, here he is in some ways closer to the eighteenth-century courtesan. The young and inexperienced can idealize the object of their love (as does Danceny with Cécile), but with time one learns that the charm was simply projected from oneself. We discover that the glamour we thought we perceived was an "illusion" (1.215), "The credulous hope of mutual minds" (216). We pass, in other words, from "Fancy's Maze" to the realm of "Truth."

> And yet 'tis hard to quit the dreams
>   Which haunt the unsuspicious soul,
> Where every nymph a goddess seems,
>   Whose eyes through rays immortal roll;
> While Fancy holds her boundless reign,
>   And all assumes a varied hue;
> When Virgins seem no longer vain,
>   And even Woman's smiles are true.
>
> ["To Romance," stanza 2]

The motif is persistent in *Don Juan*. As Johnson puts it:

> All, when Life is new,
> Commence with feelings warm, and prospects high;
>   But Time strips our illusions of their hue,
> And one by one in turn, some grand mistake
> Casts off its bright skin yearly like the snake.   [v.21]

---

2. De Laclos, *Les Liaisons dangereuses*, p. 298 (Pt. IV, Letter 134).

And he goes on to explain that "Love's the first net which spreads its deadly mesh," only to be followed by "Ambition, Avarice, Vengeance, Glory" (v.22). What is lost is blamed and regretted; what is gained is welcomed and blamed.

What is gained is called variously "apathy" (iv.4), "Indifference" (xiii.4), or "judgment" (1.215), which seems to be roughly synonymous with "insensibility." In a famous passage following hard upon the stanzas on the perils of soaring ("Nothing so difficult as a beginning," iv.1), the speaker remarks:

> As boy, I thought myself a clever fellow,
>   And wished that others held the same opinion;
> They took it up when my days grew more mellow,
>   And other minds acknowledged my dominion:
> Now my sere Fancy "falls into the yellow
>   Leaf," and Imagination droops her pinion,
> And the sad truth which hovers o'er my desk
> Turns what was once romantic to burlesque.   [iv.3]

The poet's "fall" from the romantic (associated with Fancy and Imagination) to the burlesque is, then, quite a different thing from the fall spoken of two stanzas before, where he is writing of that which comes of soaring higher than one's capacities allow. The thing to be noticed is that it is youth that is primarily the time of imagination and the imaginative flight ("While Youth's hot wishes in our red veins revel, / We know not this"; iv.2), and that loss of this capacity is part of the process of maturity. One is reminded of the Intimations Ode and the analogous complexity of Wordsworth's attitude toward the "visionary gleam" of youth and the "philosophic mind" of maturity. The poet feels the gain of seeing things as they really are; but he feels the loss, too.

The situation receives perhaps its most succinct expres-

sion in a curious little lyric that is usually dismissed with
the observation that it shows how little Byron really cared
for Mrs. Spencer Smith:

> The spell is broke, the charm is flown!
>   Thus is it with Life's fitful fever:
> We madly smile when we should groan;
>   Delirium is our best deceiver.
> Each lucid interval of thought
>   Recalls the woes of Nature's charter;
> And *He* that acts as *wise men ought*,
>   But *lives*—as Saints have died—a martyr.

Except for the distracting allusion to *Macbeth* in the second
line, this is not bad. The second quatrain is, in fact, rather
fine in its way. As we find in *Don Juan,* also, the disillusion-
ment that follows on youth is never quite complete. The
apathy is broken by upwellings of passion, sensual or otherwise. "Delirium" can momentarily blind us to the realities
of the situation; but delirium subsides (in "each lucid in-
terval of thought") and the fact of a fallen world ("the woes
of Nature's charter") is not to be escaped. Furthermore, the
man who does not permit himself to be deluded, who does
not acquiesce in spells and charms and deliriums, suffers
like a martyr for his integrity from the pain of encounter-
ing a fallen world face on.

With regard to *Don Juan* itself, and from the particular
point of view of this study, it is perhaps most useful to cite
the very interesting series of stanzas at the beginning of
Canto XIII:

> I now mean to be serious;—it is time,
>   Since Laughter now-a-days is deemed too serious;
> A jest at Vice by Virtue's called a crime,
>   And critically held as deleterious:
> Besides, the sad's a source of the sublime,

> Although, when long, a little apt to weary us;
> And therefore shall my lay soar high and solemn,
> As an old temple dwindled to a column.   [xiii.1]

In the first half of the octave the poet is expressing his uneasiness as to the way his satire had been received. A public
which so misunderstands what the poet is about (though, to
be sure, they did not have the Dedication to help them) [3]
deserves punishment in its own terms—the "sad sublime."
What Byron was accusing the public of failing to understand was the nature of satire as Pope had understood it and
as Byron continued to understand it. To them, says Byron,
there is satire, frivolous and socially irresponsible, and there
is the "high and solemn" soaring of the heroic muse, socially
and morally irreproachable. With the decay of the older tradition and the exaltation of a rather limited conception of
the sublime in the latter part of the eighteenth century, it
had been forgotten that there had been a sense in which
satire could itself be legitimately heroic.

But Byron reminds us. After a rather disorderly rehearsal
of the group of themes we have been examining (the loss of
"Romance," etc., in xiii.4–8), Byron turns his attention to a
particular artist and a particular work of art—Cervantes'
Don Quixote. Here again Byron has been greatly under-
rated. The passage is normally taken as a routine expression
of Romantic Cervantes criticism. It is a great deal more than
that. Says the poet: I am no longer subject to the powerful
feelings either of love or of hate that used to overwhelm me.
I should, however,

> . . . be very willing to redress
> Men's wrongs, and rather check than punish crimes,
> Had not Cervantes, in that too true tale
> Of Quixote, shown how all such efforts fail.

3. It was not published until 1833.

Of all tales 'tis the saddest—and more sad,
    Because it makes us smile: his hero's right,
And still pursues the right;—to curb the bad
    His only object, and 'gainst odds to fight
His guerdon: 'tis his virtue makes him mad!
    But his adventures form a sorry sight;—
A sorrier still is the great moral taught
By that real Epic unto all who have thought.

[XIII.8–9]

It is important first of all to see what the poet has done with
the concept of Romance. Previously associated with the
brief period of youthful idealism and with the soaring of
imaginative literature, it is here invested with a more specifically moral content—with

Redressing injury, revenging wrong,
    To aid the damsel and destroy the caitiff, etc.

[XIII.10]

—in other words, with the traditional idealistic content of
the romance epic. The possibility of such belief as the romance epic presupposes is destroyed by experience, especially the kind of experience dramatized in *Don Quixote,*
where the author sets out deliberately to attack the world of
romance. And in the course of satirizing romance Cervantes
has written an epic. It is a *"real* Epic," real in that it, in
contrast to the "mere Fancy" of romance, deals with reality,
or the way things really are. Like *Don Juan,* it is a creation
not of the soaring muse of high imagination, but of the
"true Muse" (VIII.1) of epic satire. But real also in the sense
of authentic, or valid. The "true Muse," as we have seen in
the Dedication, is capable of her own kind of flight. As
Byron observed in his first reply to Bowles, quoting the lines
from Pope that echo through much of *Don Juan:* " 'That
not in fancy's maze he wandered long, / But *stooped* to

Truth, and moralised his song.' He should have written 'rose to truth.' " [4]

I have suggested that *Don Juan* is like *Paradise Lost* in that, in a sense, both poems are attempts to reinterpret and recreate the epic form, and in that they are both concerned with the loss of innocence. Byron deals with the state of innocence in terms of what he calls "Romance." But he makes a rather clear distinction between two kinds of Romance. There is first the natural freshness of the unspoiled child, the Romance of, especially, Haidée. We have already seen something of its charm and its fragility. And then there is the factitious Romance, "An opium dream of too much youth and *reading* (IV.19; my italics).[5] This is the artificial innocence of a sophisticated society, a sensibility which is simply a form of self-indulgence (this is the basis of much of his attack on the "Blues"):

> Romance! disgusted with deceit,
>   Far from thy motly court I fly,
> Where Affection holds her seat,
>   And sickly Sensibility;
> Whose silly tears can never flow
>   For any pangs excepting thine;
> Who turns aside from real woe,
>   To steep in dew thy gaudy shrine.
>
> ["To Romance," stanza 5]

But this too has its charms, not the least of which is that it blends almost imperceptibly into the natural Romance of first love. Juan's boyish agonies over his love for Julia are a delightful mixture of the "natural" and the "literary." The

4. *LJ*, 5, 554. Cervantes' emphasis on the "truth" of his "chronicle" has certainly influenced Byron in his development of the motif.

5. Coleridge suggests (*Poetry, 6,* 188 n. 1) that this may refer to De Quincey or Shelley. Neither seems at all likely. I could, however, bring myself to find an allusion to Shelley in IX.73, ll. 3–5.

action of nature is obvious enough, but the literary aspect has not been adequately dealt with. Steffan, for example, has lately written of "Juan's bewildered drifting and adolescent mooning around in nature (a burlesque of Wordsworth's theories about man and nature, sts. 86–96)." [6] Now, that there are Wordsworthian echoes in the passage is certain; that they are in any useful sense a "burlesque" is at least questionable; and that the whole of 1.86–96 can be labeled Wordsworthian is simply inaccurate.

In the first place, there are only three clearly Wordsworthian lines in the whole section, the first three lines of stanza 91:

> He, Juan (and not Wordsworth), so pursued
>> His self-communion with his own high soul,
> Until his mighty heart, in its great mood,
>> Had mitigated part, though not the whole
> Of its disease.

The second and third lines are a fine piece of Wordsworth parody.[7] But that is really all there is.[8] Byron moves on to Coleridge and metaphysics, though the examples he gives have almost as little to do with Coleridge as with Wordsworth. The two stanzas on the lines from Campbell (88–9) are "romantic," to be sure, but not especially Wordsworthian. Stanza 90 seems rather a parody of the lover of courtly romance. It is closer to the *Arcadia* than to *The Prelude*. Stanza 95 informs us that Juan was reading the works of Spanish Petrarchists, while the first part of stanza 87 is a clear Petrarchan parody:

6. *Variorum, 1*, 188 n. 4.

7. Cf., for example: "And all that mighty heart is lying still" ("Westminster Bridge").

8. It is possible that stanza 94 may be a reminiscence of the famous passage on Greek myth in *The Excursion*, Bk. IV, ll. 718–44, 851–87. An argument could also be made for stanza 93, l. 2: "Longings sublime and aspirations high." But eleven lines out of eighty is not very impressive.

> Silent and pensive, idle, restless, slow,
> His home deserted for the lonely wood,
> Tormented with a wound he could not know,
> His, like all deep grief, plunged in solitude.

Which may be compared with the opening lines of one of Petrarch's most famous sonnets:

> Solo e pensoso i più deserti campi
> vo mesurando a passi tardi e lenti.
>
> [*Rime*, 39]

And, of course, the Petrarchan tradition is not silent concerning wounds from Amor's arrows and the association between love and solitude.

The literary allusions do tend to fall into two main categories which, for simplicity, we may call the "Wordsworthian" (including Campbell, Coleridge, etc.) and the "Petrarchan" (or Renaissance). It is possible the poet is alluding to these two modes when he observes that

> Nor glowing reverie, nor poet's lay,
> Could yield his spirit that for which it panted.
>
> [1.96]

"Glowing reverie" will do well enough for the flights of the Wordsworthian sublime, while "poet's lay" covers the ground of Renaissance romance. But in neither case, I would suggest, is there anything so crude as burlesque. The fact that Byron rarely mentions Wordsworth or Petrarch with much admiration does not mean that his attitude is one of simple-minded aversion. Here they participate in both the charm and the foolishness of a very young man in love. Their aptness to his mood is at once a suggestion of their justification and of their peculiar kind of limitation. They are both, in a way, immature—based on a vision which, the poet would insist, is not borne out by a dispassionate view of the way things are.

Briefly to recapitulate, we have seen the period of youth associated with "Romance," which in turn is associated with the imaginative flight and with pride. All of these motifs are found in IV.3 ("As boy, I thought myself a clever fellow"), commented on above, and they occur repeatedly in various forms throughout the poem. The pattern of association may be compared to the opening lines of Part II of the *Essay on Criticism* (Pope's point is, of course, a different one):

> Of all the Causes which conspire to blind
> Man's erring judgment, and misguide the mind,
> What the weak head with strongest bias rules,
> Is *Pride*, the never-failing vice of fools.
>
> . . . .
>
> Fired at first sight with what the Muse imparts,
> In fearless youth we tempt the heights of Arts.
>
> [ll. 201–4, 219–20]

In any case, we have here a kind of reversal of the traditional order of composition. Byron is turning his back on the "high" and "heroic" in favor of the "low" and "true." In doing so he is following Pope, who wrote his epics (the translation of Homer) first and then turned to the plain style. The Byron of *Don Juan* was criticized by *his* friends:

> You grow correct, that once with Rapture writ.

And, like his master, he replied:

> Truth guards the Poet, sanctifies the line,
> And makes immortal, Verse as mean as mine.

But Byron goes beyond Pope in his suggestion, reinforced by his juggling of traditional rhetorical concepts, of the possibility of a "real Epic," an epic that tells the truth as satire tells the truth.[9] The point need not be labored, for

9. The point that the epic poet is not strictly confined to truth is made,

these traditional concepts themselves are merely metaphoric counters the poet uses (as he does the myth of the Fall) to organize his material and to suggest the kind of attitude or world view which is the meaning of *Don Juan*.

I have hinted in passing at a comparison between *Don Juan* and the Immortality Ode. The comparison may be extended. For while Wordsworth is confessing that he has lost something personally valuable ("the visionary gleam"), he is simultaneously asserting that he has moved not only to a profounder view of human experience ("the philosophic mind") but to a higher mode of art. This is made very clear by the highly relevant epigraph—*Paulo majora canamus.* "I am now prepared to write, if not epic, something at least in a rather exalted vein." Looking at Wordsworth's works as a whole, one can think of it as a step toward the unfinished "epic" of the *Recluse.* There is a clear association of the moral (in its broadest sense) with the literary, much in the tradition of the eighteenth century.

---

for example, by Dryden in his essay "Of Heroic Plays" (quoted by Ian Jack, *Augustan Satire* (Oxford, 1952), p. 83): "An heroic poet is not tied to a bare representation of what is true, or exceedingly probable; . . . he may let himself loose to visionary objects, and to the representation of such things as depending not on sense, and therefore not to be comprehended by knowledge, may give him a freer scope for imagination" (Ker, *1*, 153). Uneasiness on this score was not, of course, new in Byron's day. In his "Essai sur la poésie épique," Voltaire, for example, has written of his own *Henriade:* "C'est pour me conformer à ce génie sage et exact qui règne dans le siècle où je vis, que j'ai choisi un héros véritable au lieu d'un héros fabuleux; que j'ai décrit des guerres réelles, et non des batailles chimériques; que je n'ai employé aucune fiction qui ne soit un image sensible de la vérité": *Œuvres complètes* (52 vols. Paris, Garnier Frères, 1877), *8*, 363. See also the invocation to the Muse, "auguste Vérité":

> Viens, parle; et s'il est vrai que la Fable autrefois
> Sut a tes fiers accents mêler sa douce voix;
> Si sa main délicate orna ta tête altière,
> Si son ombre embellit les traits de ta lumière,
> Avec moi sur tes pas permets-lui de marcher,
> Pour orner tes attraits, et non pour les cacher.

[Bk. I, ll. 15–20]

Byron's epigraph to *Don Juan* is at least equally significant. So far as I know, no one has thought to ask (in print,
at any rate) the reason for his choosing the Horatian *Difficile*—perhaps because it is too obvious, or, more likely, because of the general assumption that Byron could not mean
very much of anything. However that may be, Willis Pratt
has recently taken a step in the right direction by calling
attention to Byron's "imitation" of the Latin, the *Hints
from Horace:*[1]

> 'Tis hard to venture where our betters fail,
> Or lend fresh interest to a twice-told tale.
>
> [ll. 183–4]

It is clear that *both* verses of the couplet (Pratt carelessly
gives only the first) are intended to translate the Latin:
Difficile est proprie communia dicere (the *"tuque,* etc." is
rendered by "And yet, etc."). Interpreted in this manner,
the epigraph would be an appeal to the classic and neoclassic
doctrine of imitation, and would refer to the choice of subject. "I am, in taking up the story of Don Juan, dealing with
material that is already well-known ('a twice-told tale'). It
may be hard, but we'll see what I can do with it." The point
would be the poet's original use of traditional material.

The reading of the Lovelace manuscript, cited by Pratt, is
less clear and may possibly refer to quite a different reading
of the line:

> Whate'er the critic says or poet sings
> 'Tis no slight task to write on common things.

Here he might conceivably be interpreting *communia* as
"common topics" or "commonplaces," a reading which may
be strengthened by the association of "common things" and
"common places" in a passage of *Don Juan:*

1. *Variorum, 4,* 4. Pratt curiously "explains" the sufficiently perspicuous
reading of the printed text by the distinctly ambiguous version of the Lovelace manuscript.

This narrative is not meant for narration,
    But a mere airy and fantastic basis,
    To build up common things with common places.

[XIV.7]

And one fancies that it is not accidental when, only a few
stanzas later, the poet observes with regard to the social
group under consideration in the last cantos of the poem:

With much to excite, there's little to exalt;
    Nothing that speaks to all men and all times;
    A sort of varnish over every fault;
    A kind of common-place, even in their crimes.

[XIV.16]

Further, in light of what we have seen about the traditional
relation between the high (or "sublime") style, satire, and
truth, one is struck to observe that the English upper classes
had "A want of that *true* nature which *sublimes* / Whate'er
it shows with *Truth" (ibid.;* my italics).[2]

The point of all this comes out most clearly a little later.
In one of the invocations with which Byron decorates his
epic he announces, echoing Ariosto: [3]

Knights and Dames I sing,
    Such as the times may furnish. 'Tis a flight
Which seems at first to need no lofty wing,
    Plumed by Longinus or the Stagyrite.   [XV.25]

"Such as the times may furnish." For it is important to recall
that at this point Byron is dealing with actual "Knights and

---

2. The "sermon" of XIV.15 may be a rendering of the Horatian *sermo*,
"talk," or "satire," with its strong associations of the plain style. Pope so
renders it in *Sat.,* II.ii.9, and in the title of II.i.

3. Pratt (*Variorum, 4,* 271) cites the *Aeneid.* But Byron is much closer
to the opening lines of the *Orlando Furioso:*

Le Donne, i Cavalier'! l'arme, gli amori,
Le Cortesie, l'audaci imprese io canto.

Dames," the lords and ladies of the Regency aristocracy, and
the social equivalents, at least, of the heroes and heroines of
epic and romance. This, he says, is the best we have. If we
are to write an epic, and if, in obedience to the laws of
decorum, we choose our matter from the life of the higher
orders, it is these men and women we must deal with.
Further, if we undertake an epic we must be prepared to
"soar." But how, asks the poet, can one justify the use of
epic flight on such subjects as these?

> The difficulty lies in colouring
>   (Keeping the due proportions still in sight)
> With Nature manners which are artificial,
> And rend'ring general that which is especial.
>
> [xv.25]

Here he is making two further complaints as to the suitability for epic purposes of the material furnished by the age.
As epic poet he is obliged to meet the two demands of nature and of generality. In both cases what he is referring to
is his obligation to deal with the general, universally valid
principles of human nature, as opposed to the merely local
and accidental. But one must not ignore the unfavorable
associations of the word "artificial." The arts of civilization
(with which the poet has no argument in themselves) seem
to have got out of hand:

> In the days of old
> Men made the Manners; Manners now make men.
>
> [xv.26]

With the result that:

> With much to excite, there's little to exalt;
>   Nothing that speaks to all men and all times.
>
> [xiv.16]

I have spoken before of Byron's acute awareness of the value
and the peril of the arts of civilization. Here a new danger is

suggested; civilization has a way of reducing everybody to a dull dead level—so that the epic poet has a serious problem. He must find a hero in an unheroic age and he must attain human generality in an age occupied with factitious trifles. As Byron puts it, he

> . . . must either draw again
> Days better drawn before, or else assume
> The present, with their common-place costume.
>
> [xv.26]

Whatever the Horation *Difficile* meant at the beginning of *Don Juan,* it has now come to refer to the commonplace humanity set before the prospective epic poet of the early nineteenth century.

Much earlier in the poem, at the height of the Haidée idyll, Byron's island laureate had sung:

> The heroic lay is tuneless now—
>   The heroic bosom beats no more!
> And must thy Lyre, so long divine,
> Degenerate into hands like mine?
>
> ["The Isles of Greece," stanza 5]

And in so speaking he is only echoing what Byron himself had said many years before in the first of the "Turkish Tales." Byron begins *The Giaour* with a meditation on the heroic days of Greece, commenting on its present degradation. Greece is as beautiful as ever, but the moral and spiritual quality of her people has decayed:

> What can he tell who treads thy shore?
>   No legend of thine olden time,
> No theme on which the Muse might soar
> High as thine own in days of yore,
>   When man was worthy of thy clime.
>
> [*The Giaour,* ll. 142–6]

Here again the motif of the connection between moral elevation and poetic sublimity. Greece now presents no material for those poetic flights for which her literature is uniquely distinguished. So what shall I write of modern Greece? Not an epic, surely; but a "Turkish Tale." And not even a whole tale; merely "disjointed fragments." The land is Greece, but the principal characters are Turk and Frank. Only the conspicuously frequent and extended "Homeric" similes may remind the reader of the heroic tradition.[4]

He arrives at a somewhat different solution of the problem posed by a colorless aristocracy:

> We'll do our best to make the best on't:—March!
> 　March, my Muse! If you cannot fly, yet flutter;
> And when you may not be sublime, be arch,
> 　Or starch, as are the edicts statesmen utter.
> We surely may find something worth research:
> 　Columbus found a new world in a cutter,
> Or brigantine, or pink, of no great tonnage,
> While yet America was in her non-age.　　[xv.27]

Here he is simply granting the impossibility of treating his polished patricians as traditional epic heroes. The soaring heroic muse will be forced to "flutter" along. The image is a conventional one for the failure of imaginative *essor*. The word is so used, for example, in the introductory essay to Gifford's *Juvenal*. Of the "heroic" satirist he observes: "His element was that of the eagle, 'descent and fall to him were adverse,' and, indeed, he never appears more awkward than when he flutters, or rather waddles, along the ground."[5] It will be, as it were, a "low" epic. And then again he presents

4. Notice especially ll. 68–103, 388–421, 422–38, 505–16, 620–42, 661–4, 945–50, 951–6, 1159–66. Notice also ll. 640–2, where the pastoral locale is given over to violence.

5. William Gifford, tr., *The Satires of Decimus Junius Juvenalis* (London, 1806), p. lxvi.

us with one of his most valuable metaphors of the nature of the "real" epic, that of the voyage of exploration. He is harking back to the passage "In the wind's eye I have sailed, etc." (x.4) which I have discussed in Chapter 2, and to the fine stanzas only a few pages earlier:

'Tis strange—but true; for Truth is always strange—
   Stranger than fiction: if it could be told,
How much would novels gain by the exchange!
   How differently the World would men behold!
How oft would Vice and Virtue places change!
   The new world would be nothing to the old,
If some Columbus of the moral seas
Would show mankind their Souls' antipodes.

What "antres vast and deserts idle," then,
   Would be discovered in the human soul!
What icebergs in the hearts of mighty men,
   With self-love in the centre as their Pole!

[XIV.101–2]

Here he is appealing to the "romantic" associations (or even epic, if one thinks of the *Odyssey*, the *Télémaque*, or, especially, the *Lusiads*) of the voyage of adventure. It is glamorous, and it is in search of truth, a truth which Byron presents as not only more valuable but more "romantic" than fiction. In words that remind us of the way he has created a subjective version of the romance-epic in *Childe Harold's Pilgrimage: A Romaunt* (where the subtitle indicates the genre against which Byron's poem is constantly to be compared), we learn that the voyage is to be into the heart of social man.[6]

6. With reference to this metaphor of the voyage, compare the following lines from the suppressed stanzas on Brougham (*Poetry, 6*, 69 n.):

I'm sorry thus to probe a wound so raw—
   But, then, as Bard my duty to Mankind,
For warning to the rest, compels these raps—
As Geographers lay down a Shoal in Maps.

As far, at least, as the incomplete poem we possess is concerned, the voyage comes to its climax in the English cantos.
And while it is always well in discussing this section to bear
in mind that it is not finished and that we do not know how
Byron was going to develop the situation, a few generalizations may perhaps be hazarded. In the first place, it is the
only section of the poem which actually deals with a social
group, and thus is the only episode that would really fit in
any proposed plan of treating the characteristic absurdities
of the various peoples of Europe.[7] And it is this section in
which he seems to be making his most earnest attempt at
dramatizing the possibility of "real Epic." [8] The section is,
then, conspicuous not only for its treatment of society and
for the number and importance of its evocations of the
world of classical epic, but also for the persistence with
which it reminds us of the difficulties involved in the notion
of reality.

The English cantos, in fact, begin with a consideration of
"what is":

7. See the letter to Murray, Feb. 16, 1821 (*LJ*, 5, 242).

8. There is some reason to suspect that the poet is setting up the situation in epic terms. After commenting on the something undefined that Lord
Henry lacked (Byron displays an almost Jamesean fondness for the indefinable in these English cantos), the poet makes a striking allusion to the
action of the *Iliad:*

> Still there was something wanting, as I've said—
>   That undefinable *"Je ne sçais quoi,"*
> Which, for what I know, may of yore have led
>   To Homer's Iliad, since it drew to Troy
> The Greek Eve, Helen, from the Spartan's bed;
>   Though on the whole, no doubt, the Dardan boy
> Was much inferior to King Menelaus:—
> But thus it is some women will betray us.   [XIV.72]

I am strongly of the opinion that Byron had the progress of the episode
worked out in his own mind, and it seems at least possible that he was
preparing to draw on the epic tradition rather more specifically than in
the earlier cantos. He may have been amusing himself with the idea of an
Iliad of which Paris is the hero. And evidently he would have continued
to make use of the metaphor of the Fall ("The Greek Eve, Helen").

When Bishop Berkeley said "there was no matter,"
  And proved it—'twas no matter what he said:
They say his system 'tis in vain to batter,
  Too subtle for the airiest human head;
And yet who can believe it? I would shatter
  Gladly all matters, down to stone or lead,
Or adamant, to find the world a spirit,
And wear my head, denying that I wear it.

What a sublime discovery 'twas to make the
  Universe universal egotism,
That all's ideal—*all ourselves!*—I'll stake the
  World (be it what you will) that *that's* no schism.
Oh Doubt!—if thou be'st Doubt, for which some
      take thee,
  But which I doubt extremely—thou sole prism
Of the Truth's rays, spoil not my draught of spirit!
Heaven's brandy, though our brain can hardly bear it.

                                              [XI.1–2]

The grasp of metaphysics may not be impressive, but the
edginess of the passage is of more than biographical interest.
The poet wants to base his epic solidly on reality, and he
wants to make a point of the fact. And while he is hardly
obliged to outline an ontology, it is well at least to forestall
objections of excessive naïveté by indicating an awareness of
the complexity of the problem. Furthermore, it is to his
interest (as well as to his taste) to undermine any systematic
formulation of reality, to set system against system (XIV.1–2),
and to exalt the primacy of that immediate experience
(what he sometimes calls "fact," or "existence") of which
the poet is a peculiarly authoritative spokesman. And
finally, the question of reality is important to the poem's
social comment.

    To restrict ourselves for the moment to this one canto
(XI), the introductory stanzas on metaphysics are followed by

the episode on Shooter's Hill. Here there is not only an exposure of the seamy side of an ostentatiously free and moral nation, but there is accomplished playing with the notion of heroism (20) and the "great man" (19) much in the manner of Fielding in *Jonathan Wild*. "He from the world had cut off a great man, etc." The difference between a footpad and statesman, it is implied, is largely a matter of social convention (cf. the "sea-sollicitor" Lambro). This is followed immediately by an octave on "Groves, so called as being void of trees"—commenting on a characteristic manifestation of lower middle-class gentility, where the charm and elegance is largely a matter of names. Stanzas 35–7 are concerned with lying. Here the attitude is more complex. Politicians "live by lies, yet dare not boldly lie," in contrast to women, who "won't / Or can't do otherwise than lie—but do it / So well, the very Truth seems falsehood to it" (36). Furthermore, a lie is simply "The truth in masquerade," and lying is indispensable to society as at present constituted (37). Then he undertakes to show the reality of social life, the vicissitudes of the great in their "earthly Paradise of *Or Molu*" (67–75). The brilliant *ubi sunt* and *carpe diem* stanzas with which the canto ends are concluded with some cynical lines on the "play" of life:

> "Life's a poor player,"—then "play out the play,
> Ye villains!" and above all keep a sharp eye
>   Much less on what you do than what you say:
>   Be hypocritical, be cautious, be
> Not what you *seem*, but always what you *see*.   [XI.86]

Byron exploits the possibilities of the play or masquerade theme with some skill. In the passage just quoted he is recommending the deliberate adoption of a role if one wants to advance in society. It is important not to "be oneself" ("what you *seem*"), but the self society expects you to be ("what you *see*"). It is the mingled glamour, pathos, and absurdity of this situation that Byron is trying to suggest when he observes:

> Sometimes, indeed, like soldiers off parade,
>   They break their ranks and gladly leave the drill;
> But then the roll-call draws them back afraid,
>   And they must be or seem what they *were:* still
> Doubtless it is a brilliant masquerade.   [xiv.17]

These Regency aristocrats caught in their social roles call to mind Sartre's waiter "playing at being a waiter." The very typicality or lack of individuality in the list of guests at Norman Abbey is to the point. He interrupts his catalogue deliberately to remark:

> Good company's a chess-board—there are kings,
>   Queens, bishops, knights, rooks, pawns; the
>   World's a game;
> Save that the puppets pull at their own strings,
>   Methinks gay Punch hath something of the same.
>   [xiii.89]

It is the inhuman, mechanical rigidity and limitation of personality that seems most profoundly to disturb the poet. In terms of the "Ode to a Lady," this is clearly a world in which love is "a bondage or a trade":

> But coming young from lands and scenes romantic,
>   Where lives, not lawsuits, must be risked for Passion,
> And Passion's self must have a spice of frantic,
>   Into a country where 'tis half a fashion,
> Seemed to him half commercial, half pedantic.
>   [xii.68]

And Byron delights in references to lawsuits and damages.[9]

But this is too simple to do justice to Byron. The *ubi sunt* and *carpe diem* stanzas toward the end of Canto xi (76–86)

9. For example, xi.89; xii.65, 68.

remind us that *Don Juan* is a poem that is concerned with
time and with the changes that take place in time, with the
emphasis falling heavily on the feeling of loss. With this is
conjoined one stanza on the "business" of love and marriage
in England (89) and three associating the poet's truthfulness
and poetic sublimity (87, 89–90):

> Thus far, go forth, thou Lay, which I will back
> Against the same given quantity of rhyme,
>   For being as much the subject of attack
> As ever yet was any work sublime,
>   By those who love to say that white is black.
> So much the better!—I may stand alone,
> But would not change my free thoughts for a throne.
>
>   [XI.90]

Now one of the points I am most concerned to make
about Byron's method in *Don Juan* is that it is always extremely important to notice what he is associating with
what. For Byron achieves some of his finest effects by simple
thematic association (such as that of love with war, dealt
with in Chapter 3). It may be instructive, therefore, to examine this particular thematic group—time, love, business,
and the sublimity of poetic truth.

One reason why it is especially useful to an enjoyment of
Don Juan at least unconsciously to have made this particular association is that the poet appears to pick it up and
elaborate it at the beginning of the next canto. And the beginning of Canto XII marks a turning point of some importance in the development of the poem.

We hear first of all about the speaker's age. He is "middle-
aged," and he doesn't like it much:

> Too old for Youth,—too young, at thirty-five,
>   To herd with boys, or hoard with good threescore,—
> I wonder people should be left alive;

But since they are, that epoch is a bore:
Love lingers still, although 'twere late to wive:
    And as for other love, the illusion's o'er;
And Money, that most pure imagination,
Gleams only through the dawn of its creation.   [XII.2]

Now that the "illusion" of romantic love is no longer possible (cf. 1.215–16), the only charm that seems to lie ahead is money and the making of money—money being as specifically associated with age and experience as romantic love has been with youth and innocence. And while the poet has been generous in his appreciation of the charms of love, there is clearly something to be said for money, too.

"Love rules the Camp, the Court, the Grove,—for Love
    Is Heaven, and Heaven is Love:"—so sings the bard;
Which it were rather difficult to prove
    (A thing with poetry in general hard).
Perhaps there may be something in "the Grove,"
    At least it rhymes to "Love:" but I'm prepared
To doubt (no less than landlords of their rental)
If "Courts" and "Camps" be quite so sentimental.

But if Love don't, *Cash* does, and Cash alone:
    Cash rules the Grove, and fells it too besides;
Without cash, camps were thin, and courts were none;
    Without cash, Malthus tells you—"take no brides."
So Cash rules Love the ruler, on his own
    High ground, as virgin Cynthia sways the tides.
                                            [XII.13–14]

Money is not only in itself an object of excitement and romance (see the analysis of XII.8 in Chapter 5); it "rules Love the ruler." And the tone is no longer, in this respect, quite that of the Ode. This may not be the way the poet would have it if he had a choice. But he is not merely bitter about the situation. And if the tone is not one of simple amusement, neither is it one of savage satire. "Thus it is," says the speaker. Money is not romantic, perhaps—but in a sense it is. Furthermore, if love is an illusion, money in any case is very real. And the converting of its hard unglamorous reality into a thing of curious beauty is of clear relevance to an "epic" poet who is concerned with writing truth. The notion of the rule of love over human affairs is, says the speaker, "poetic," and poetry tells lies. But the poet of the "truthful Muse," engaged in writing a "real Epic," must be rigorously honest without ceasing to be a poet. Hence the point of the tour de force at the beginning of Canto XII, creating for us a vision of that inevitable change in the life of every man from youth to age—and a vision which presents mutability as more than merely loss. The poet faces the hard facts of experience and finds them not lacking in their own kind of charm.

The point is of clear importance in the working out of the plot. Its elaboration, in fact, seems to be the principal action of the English cantos. For if the world of the English cantos is in some ways analogous to that of the Ode, it is equally clear that a "Lady" is being prepared with whom Juan is to become involved in an affair in every sense more perilous than any of his previous adventures. Adeline is explicitly said to be "The fair most fatal Juan ever met" (XIII.12). And that is clearly the point of Byron's insistence on the strength of passion of which apparently cold English ladies are capable (XII.76–7), most notably in the elaborate conceits of the bottle of frozen champagne and the "North-West Passage / Unto the glowing India of the Soul" (XIII.36–8), referring specifically to Adeline. She is, says the poet, like

> . . . a bottle of champagne
> Frozen into a very vinous ice,
>   Which leaves few drops of that immortal rain,

Yet in the very centre, past all price,
  About a liquid glassful will remain;
  And this is stronger than the strongest grape
  Could e'er express in its expanded shape.   [XIII.37]

The point to be noticed is this: the apparent coldness and
the unfavorable social circumstances are seen as contrib-
uting factors to the intensity of their love, even as the passion of the Lady of the Ode was refined and made more intense by her own "coldness" and the circumstances which
rendered her love a "guilty" one.[1]

The point is worth laboring. Neither the image of ice
nor the ideal of restraint has been invested with much
grandeur in the course of the poem. We have seen ice in
VII.1–2 as a "wasteland" image over which flashes the aurora
borealis of poetry. And the image has been used in the English cantos to express some of the less pleasant aspects of
English society (XII.25, 41, 72). But the attitude toward restraint has been ambiguous throughout. In the discussion of
Juan's education, for example, we are led to suppose that
the boy was being excessively held down:

For half his days were passed at church, the other
Between his tutors, confessor, and mother.   [I.49]

  They tamed him down amongst them: to destroy
His natural spirit not in vain they toiled,
    At least it seemed so.   [I.50]

The qualifying clause reminds us, however, of the futility
of all repression. "Nature," evidently, will out. See the can-
celed final couplet to II.10.[2]

But even as he criticizes Donna Inez for being overly re-

1. This point has been skillfully developed by Ernest J. Lovell, Jr., in his
essay "Irony and Image in Byron's *Don Juan*," in Thorpe, Baker, and
Weaver, eds., *The Major English Romantic Poets*, p. 139.

2.   Their manners mending, and their morals curing,
              She taught them to suppress their vice—and urine.

pressive in bringing up her son, he is also taking her to task
for being too lax:

> Oh ye! who teach the ingenuous youth of nations,
>   Holland, France, England, Germany, or Spain,
> I pray ye flog them upon all occasions—
>   It mends their morals, never mind the pain:
> The best of mothers and of educations
>   In Juan's case were but employed in vain,
> Since, in a way that's rather of the oddest, he
> Became divested of his native modesty.
>
> Had he but been placed at a public school,
>   In the third form, or even in the fourth,
> His daily task had kept his fancy cool,
>   At least, had he been nurtured in the North;
> Spain may prove an exception to the rule,
>   But then exceptions always prove its worth—
> A lad of sixteen causing a divorce
> Puzzled his tutors very much, of course.[3]   [II.1–2]

This apparent contradiction serves more than one function. In the first place it brings out the instability of Donna
Inez. More important is the suggestion that the alternate
severity and laxity tended to cancel each other out (like
Fielding's Thwackum and Square), so that when Don Juan
goes out into the world he has to deal with it (like Tom
Jones) with his own natural resources. The analogy with the
sinking ship with "all distinction gone" (II.44) is clear

3. Cf. 1.25:

> A little curly-headed, good-for-nothing,
>   And mischief-making monkey from his birth;
> His parents ne'er agreed except in doting
>   Upon the most unquiet imp on earth;
> Instead of quarrelling, had they been both in
>   Their senses, they'd have sent young master forth
> To school, or had him soundly whipped at home,
> To teach him manners for the time to come.

enough. Both the shipwreck and the mode of Juan's education permit the boy to exercise his own natural capacities
unhelped (or hindered) by education or by institutional
supports. And finally, there is the suggestion of the value in
discipline itself.

Already in the third chapter I have commented on the
speaker's attitude toward the repression of emotion, observing that he often seems to think of it as a purely physical
phenomenon, like steam confined and causing an explosion.
This is an essential part of that post of detached objectivity
which is one of the most obvious qualities of the *persona* in
Don Juan. He needs it, of course, to make good his claims
of speaking truth. He watches, he describes, he sympathizes;
but he is reluctant to judge. It is one of the things about
Don Juan that makes it seem so curiously French. If he is
quite merciless in following out the consequences of passion
it is not because he acknowledges religious or philosophical
sanctions for morality, but because in his own experience
as man of the world he has learned that, like it or not, passion *does* end in disaster. It may be worth it, but the consequences are clear and, apparently, inexorable. It is for this
reason that he so emphasizes his own worldliness and sophistication. He needs it to validate a particular kind of statement. What might seem the almost Calvinist morality of
Don Juan is not really morality at all in the usual sense. At
least it claims not to be. It presents itself as the observation
of a man who is able to offer impressive evidence of his objectivity and first-hand knowledge. The speaker's insistence
on his own sophistication may be compared to that of the
Ode, or of Donne's "The Relique."

For, as I have already suggested, there is a notable change
of emphasis in the course of *Don Juan*. I have ventured to
compare the poem with *Paradise Lost* in that both "epics"
are concerned with the loss of innocence. And in the early
cantos this loss is lamented with some passion: "No more—

no more—Oh! never more on me!" But even as the loss is lamented, the fact of gain is at least asserted:

> The illusion's gone for ever, and thou art
>   Insensible, I trust, but none the worse,
> And in thy stead I've got a deal of judgment,
>   Though Heaven knows how it ever found a lodgment.
>
> [1.215]

And as the poem develops, the emphasis is much less on what has been lost than on what has been gained—on the dangers and opportunities.

> Adversity is the first path to Truth:
>   He who hath proved War—Storm—or Woman's rage,
> Whether his winters be eighteen or eighty,
>   Hath won the experience which is deemed so weighty.
>
> [XII.50]

Experience is now not so much a thing to be lamented as a thing to test oneself against and a means of arriving at something that may be called truth. The fall is "fortunate."

Early in the first canto there is a stanza (part of which I have already quoted in another context) in which the speaker comments on Juan's boy-love for Julia:

> Silent and pensive, idle, restless, slow,
>   His home deserted for the lonely wood,
> Tormented with a wound he could not know,
>   His, like all deep grief, plunged in solitude:
> I'm fond myself of solitude or so,
>   But then, I beg it may be understood,
> By solitude I mean a Sultan's (not
> A Hermit's), with a haram for a grot.   [1.87]

I dare say this is usually taken as simply another example of Byronic digression (or of showing off). It is, in fact, highly relevant. The point of the stanza, and a point that it makes very well, is the enormous gap between the speaker and the protagonist; for both taken together form the third great unifying device of the poem (along with the myth of the Fall and the theory of the styles), and the relations between them are central to an understanding of *Don Juan*. At the beginning of the poem, as the quoted stanza dramatizes, there is a great gulf between them. On the one hand we have the gauche adolescent suffering awkwardly through his first affair. Looking down on him affectionately from Olympian heights is the worldly speaker—who calls attention to his worldliness at this point for very important reasons. One way of defining the action of *Don Juan* would be to say that it consists of a process of gradually narrowing the gap between speaker and protagonist. For if Juan falls from innocence, in the course of the poem he rises to the level of the speaker. The gain is not unequivocal and the process is far from complete when the poem ends. But it is impossible not to feel that the English cantos mark a clear turning point in the development of the poem. By the end the categories of innocence and experience have become largely irrelevant. The very iciness of the world has become a source of potential charm.

All of which, I hope, may suggest that it is very easy to limit too narrowly the scope of *Don Juan*. I am unable to persuade myself that in it Byron is merely "giggling and making giggle," exposing cant, or, especially, writing a treatise on appearance and reality (three popular and representative schools of thought). From this point of view the problem with regard to *Don Juan* is in many ways strongly suggestive of problems raised by *Don Quixote*—and it may have been an implicit awareness of some of this that led Byron to compose his stanzas on the "real Epic." In the course of its long history *Don Quixote* has suffered from two radical interpretations—one seeing it as a farce-satire and the other as a kind of exercise in metaphysics. I think that of the two serious distortions the first is far truer to Cervantes. It is important to perceive, as Erich Auerbach has pointed out, that the whole tone and temper of *Don Quixote* forbids incursions into the ontologically problematic.[4] It is simply untrue that one is aware of metaphysical depths opening before one, or that in the shuffling of "levels of reality" in Part II either Cervantes or the reader is ever for a moment uncertain as to "where" reality actually "is." The point of view may be, in a way, naïve, but in other and more interesting ways it is very refined indeed. And if Cervantes is not Calderon, *Don Juan* is not *The Tempest*. And the point of view of Byron's poem is susceptible of the same charge of naïveté (a charge which one can endure in the company of Cervantes). This is not to say that either *Don Quixote* or *Don Juan* is, as a vision, simple. It is rather that in both Byron and Cervantes the complexity is in the quality of the acquiescence in a world which is, for the most part, simply given. It is because *Don Juan* is, in the sense this study has been an attempt to define, an act of acquiescence in that real world that it can claim to be, like *Don Quixote*, a "real Epic." [5]

4. Erich Auerbach, "The Enchanted Dulcinea," *Mimesis. The Representation of Reality in Western Literature* (Princeton Univ. Press, 1953), pp. 334–58, esp. 351 ff.

5. Notice that, just at the moment when the issue becomes thematically crucial (after the disastrous end of the affair with Haidée), Byron gives us extended depictions of reaction to adversity in the narrative of the buffo (iv.81–9) and the description of the captives (v.7–9), and in the speeches of Johnson (v.13–25).

Chapter 5

"CARELESSLY I SING"

TOWARD THE END of Canto VIII the poet announces:

> Reader! I have kept my word,—at least so far
>   As the first Canto promised. You have now
> Had sketches of Love—Tempest—Travel—War,—
>   All very accurate, you must allow,
> And *Epic,* if plain truth should prove no bar;
>   For I have drawn much less with a long bow
> Than my forerunners. Carelessly I sing,
> But Phœbus lends me now and then a string.
>
> [VIII.138]

It seems that he is taking particular pains at the end of the two "war cantos" to remind us of the claim his poem has been making to be epic. And the terms are such as should be familiar to us. Not only have his "sketches of Love—Tempest—Travel—War" presumably fulfilled the external thematic and episodic requirements of the epic form but, we are told, they are "All very accurate." The comment is especially justified at this point, of course, since the cantos on the Siege of Ismail follow their source (Castelnau's *Histoire de la nouvelle Russie*) with a fidelity unusual even in Byron. And there is the highly characteristic uneasiness

124

as to the compatibility of accuracy and epic: "if plain truth should prove no bar." He accordingly reminds us that while he emphatically considers himself in the line of epic poets, he is an epic poet in the plain style: "I have drawn much less with a long bow / Than my forerunners." There is an explicit association between content and style, the truth with which the poem deals and the manner in which it deals with it. The "carelessness" of his song is connected with the truth it is to express. Hence the chatty, conversational manner, the easy, informal tone which gains much of its significance from an implied contrast with the grand manner of epic—especially that manner as communicated by Milton and Pope.

But if it is accurate to say that this is an epic which is plain in manner and veracious in content, the emphasis can be reversed. This is what happens at the end of the stanza. The manner is simple and the matter the simple facts, but at the same time it is epic. It claims the inspiration of the Leader of the Muses: "Phœbus lends me now and then a string." The stylistic problem of *Don Juan* should, then, be clear enough. The manner must be informal and conversational ("careless"), a deliberate scandal in terms of the traditional concepts of epic style. But while, as I have pointed out, the primary reference of stylistic level is to intensity of tone, the poet will be well-advised to provide a rhetorical organization that will facilitate our acceptance of the epic pretensions of the poem. It is, then, the more specifically rhetorical aspects of the art of *Don Juan* with which I shall concern myself in this final chapter.

Just as it is essential for the content of the poem to seem random and rambling when in fact it is relentlessly coherent and unified, the style of the poem itself presents a striking combination of the conversationally offhand and the elaborately rhetorical. Now perhaps the simplest way of giving form to a stanza of *ottava rima,* and a way highly congenial to a lover of Pope, would be to treat the eight lines as four rhythmically independent units—as a kind of unrhymed heroic couplets. Byron sometimes does this:

> But Juan was no casuist, nor had pondered
> 　　Upon the moral lessons of mankind:
> Besides, he had not seen of several hundred
> 　　A lady altogether to his mind.
> A little *blasé*—'tis not to be wondered
> 　　At, that his heart had got a tougher rind:
> And though not vainer from his past success,
> No doubt his sensibilities were less.　　[XII.81]

More often, however, he will prefer a freer movement, tightening up only in the final couplet:

> While things were in abeyance, Ribas sent
> 　　A courier to the Prince, and he succeeded
> In ordering matters after his own bent;
> 　　I cannot tell the way in which he pleaded,
> But shortly he had cause to be content.
> 　　In the mean time, the batteries proceeded,
> And fourscore cannon on the Danube's border
> Were briskly fired and answered in due order.
>
> 　　　　　　　　　　　　　　　　　　[VII.38]

The tone of this stanza is studiously unpoetic ("careless"), helping persuade us of the poet's objectivity and scrupulous regard for truth ("I cannot tell . . ."). It is only in the unbroken movement of the concluding couplet that the conscientiously prosy movement is resolved. But the couplet does more than that. In its brisk pace, vigorous rhymes, and circular movement it provides a precise rhetorical equivalent to the efficient futility of the cannonade. (It might be worth noting that the stanza does not appear to be a close translation of the source; but it is made to sound as if it were).

But Byron has a virtuoso mastery of the elements of his

octave (the very fact that it is so generally unrecognized is a kind of tribute to his unobtrusive control), and he is particularly resourceful in his use of the final couplet:

> And that still keeping up the old connection,
>> Which Time had lately rendered much more chaste,
> She took his lady also in affection,
>> And certainly this course was much the best:
> She flattered Julia with her sage protection,
>> And complimented Don Alfonso's taste;
> And if she could not (who can?) silence scandal,
> At least she left it a more slender handle.   [1.67]

The octave is arranged in couplets, with a pause or full stop at the end of every line. There are no strong internal pauses to retard the speed—he is being gossipy here—or, to look at it in another way, to relieve the monotony. This throws a great deal of weight on the final couplet (all the greater because the stanza is grammatically and rhetorically an extension of the previous one), which must provide a satisfactory resolution. And it seems to me no denigration of Byron's skill to point out that the devices used are simple (not, after all, the same thing as "easy"). They are devices of elementary manipulation of rhythm and sound-pattern:

> And if she could not (who can?) silence scandal,
> At least she left it a more slender handle.

The rhythm is broken first of all by the series of five consecutive stresses in the first line—"could not (who can?) si-." Rhythmically (as opposed to metrically) the first line ends with two strong spondees followed by two trochees (which gain force by the alliterating *s's* and the repetition of the *l's* and *n's*): "could not (who can?) silence scandal." [1]

1. I should scan it:

And if she could not (who can?) silence scandal.

In terms of traditional scansion there are no "trochees" in the line. At the

The *l* is picked up again in the second line, this time in the alliterating accented syllables of the introductory iambs. The conclusion of the second line parallels the first, ending in two dissyllables forming strong trochees.[2] The first ("slender") picks up the *s* from the conclusion of the preceding line, as well as the *n*, which occurs again in "handle." In addition, the two words share voiced dentals (*d*) between a nasal (*n*) and a liquid (*r, l*)—the point of which is to suggest how Byron builds up his couplet acoustically and rhythmically, endowing it with the substance required by its rhetorical function as the climax of fourteen lines of chit-chat. It is strong enough for its purpose and yet discreet enough not to make one conscious of the presence of rhetoric in a passage where our awareness of it would spoil the gossipy effect. For one of the most important manifestations of the *persona* is the rattle-brained chatter-box—so putting us off guard when the thrust comes ("I'm sure I mean no harm").[3] It is among the richest sources of Byronic irony.

While criticism of Byron is well supplied with vague observations about "energy" and "force," it seems never to have been adequately appreciated that Lord Byron had a real genius for the handling of rhythm. The couplet we have just been examining is quiet and unobtrusive, and rhythmically accomplished; there is no excuse to suppose

---

risk, however, of initial misunderstanding, I have in this chapter sometimes used the traditional metrical feet to describe what are not always strictly metrical units. If I knew of a simpler way of making this kind of point I should use it.

2. I should scan this second line:

$$\times \; / \; | \; \times \; / \; | \times \; / \; | \quad \frown \quad | \times \; / \; | \times$$
At least she left it a more slender handle.

Perhaps the relative intensity of "more" (felt rhythmically as the third beat of an anapest—the accent on *a* is honorific) makes it easier to feel the last two words as rhythmical units.

3. IX.7.

that Byron shines only in the loud passages. Both in tone and in manner he has much greater range than is usually granted (*Childe Harold* has suffered especially from the stubborn insistence on always hearing Byron shout). In neither of the next two stanzas I shall be considering is there any denunciation or beating of the breast; but both are brilliant specimens of rhythmical modulation, and both are characteristically Byronic:

> At one o'clock the wind with sudden shift
>   Threw the ship right into the trough of the sea,
> Which struck her aft, and made an awkward rift,
>   Started the stern-post, also shattered the
> Whole of her stern-frame, and ere she could lift
>   Herself from out her present jeopardy,
> The rudder tore away: 'twas time to sound
> The pumps, and there were four feet water found.
>
> [II.27]

No small part of the effect of this stanza is the result of Byron's close following of the fine vigorous prose of his source (it is the work of the "truthful Muse"):

> Night came on worse than the day had been; and a *sudden shift of wind,* about midnight, *threw the ship into the trough of the sea, which struck her aft, tore away the rudder, started the stern-post, and shattered the whole of her stern-frame. The pumps were immediately sounded,* and in the course of a few minutes the water had increased to *four feet.*[4]

Since Byron has already informed us in the previous stanza (26) that it was night, he can omit the first part of the passage. "One o'clock" is both more definite and less obviously melodramatic than "about midnight." It also makes possible a *w* alliteration which, in context and in conjunction with

4. *Poetry, 6,* 88–9 n. The italics are the editor's.

the concluding alliterating sibilants ("*s*udden *s*hift"), composes a line of effective auditory mimesis (onomatopoeia)—the whistling and the soughing of the wind. The fact that four of the five accented syllables bear the further weight of alliteration emphasizes the strictly regular beat (metrical and rhythmical stresses coincide almost exactly). This is important, because the verse of auditory is followed immediately by a verse of rhythmical mimesis: "Threw the ship right into the trough of the sea." Byron has taken the passage intact from his source, with the addition of an adverb. That the metrical irregularity of the line is intended to mimic the tossing motion is clear. The spondaic second foot (strengthened by the half-rhyme of "shift" with "ship," cutting across the line divisions, adding to the feeling of impetuosity) and the (whatever it may be metrically) anapestic rhythm of the end of the line ("-to the trough of the sea") [5] help to create as nice a specimen of neoclassical sound and sense as one could hope to find. The addition of the adverb may facilitate our feeling the end of the line as strongly anapestic.

The third line—while providing a welcome reassurance as to the metrical norm from which the variations of the preceding verse and (especially) the following verses derive much of their force—also contributes a mimetically valuable strong caesura, emphasized by the internal half-rhyme of "aft" and "rift." It is in the next two lines, however, that the rhythmical mimesis becomes most interesting (the first line and a half, except for the connective, is taken over unchanged from the source):

> Started the stern-post, also shattered the
> Whole of her stern-frame, and ere she could lift . . .

5. For purposes of scansion I should read it:

Threw the ship right into the trough of the sea.

Rhythmically the first line is suspended between two almost-rhyming dactyls: "Started the . . . shattered the." [6] This device, with remarkable economy, gives both shape and impetus to the line. It is rushed into the next line, passing easily over the very light rhyme-word ("the"), and the whole rhythmical unit is finished off with a repetition of the two strong stresses that had concluded the first phrase ("stern-post . . . stern-frame"). The passage has an almost jazzy quality about it. And the effect is all the greater not only because of the resistance of the metrical norm (which has been impressed on us in the previous line), but also, perhaps, from the invitation to special emphasis one may discover in the piling up of sibilants. All this is very subjective, but as I feel the passage there is a kind of tension between the forces pushing the movement forward and those tending to retard it that helps make these lines a particularly effective imitation of physical thrust and resistance and final overthrow. The halting conclusion of the line ("and ere she could lift") moves us into the metrically regular sixth line (but still with a weak rhyme: "jeopardy"), and the whole movement is concluded in the inexorable "sound/found" rhyme of the couplet. The feeling of helplessness in the face of natural forces has received less effective expression than in these lines of Byron's.

But Byron's rhythmic gifts are not apparent only in passages of imitation (or better, in passages imitative of external, as opposed to internal, events) and in reworkings of source materials. The action of the second specimen is the expression of a state of mind, and so far as I know (aside from the precedent of Sir Epicure Mammon) it is entirely original. It is part of the brilliantly Augustan praise of

6. Started the stern-post, also shattered the.

The final accent is merely a tribute to the metrical pattern. It is obviously very weak; and the rhythmic effect is dactylic.

avarice at the beginning of Canto XII. Byron is speaking of the miser:

> He is your only poet;—Passion, pure
>   And sparkling on from heap to heap, displays
> *Possessed,* the ore, of which *mere hopes* allure
>   Nations athwart the deep: the golden rays
> Flash up in ingots from the mine obscure:
>   On him the Diamond pours its brilliant blaze,
> While the mild Emerald's beam shades down the dies
> Of other stones, to soothe the miser's eyes.   [XII.8]

It is the first three lines with which we are especially concerned. And it should be clear that the same rhythmical devices are being used here as in the stanza just analyzed. The *s's* and *t's* of the earlier passage are paralleled by the *p's* and *s's* of this one. The push of the enjambment has again to contend with the opportunities for declamation presented by the alliterating words, while the movement from line three to line four is retarded by the half-rhyme of "the ore" and "allure" (there is, in fact, a rhythmical and acoustical balancing of *"Possessed,* the ore . . . *mere hopes* allure" that is reminiscent of the "Started the . . . shattered the" of the first passage). There is again, in short, the same tension between push and resistance that we have seen used to such fine effect in the earlier passage. Byron is seeking rhythmically to validate the romance with which, as I have observed, he chooses at this moment to invest the miser. For, as I read it, the passage is an element in the poem's shift in emphasis from innocence to experience, of which "avarice" is a powerful symbol.

After the vigorous rhythms of the opening lines, the octave resolves itself in five lines phrased with the most elegant formality. The formal center of the section is line 6: "On him the Diamond pours its brilliant blaze." Reading from this line in either direction, one finds a line without caesura in enjambment with two iambs—followed after a caesura by three iambs at the beginning and end of their respective lines. The phrasing is exquisitely balanced.[7] A proper reading of the lines will make it clear that the effect is not merely visual; for if the poet is carefully shifting the weight of the poem toward the pole of experience, he himself is experienced enough not to be simple-minded about it. And the most appropriate form of irony is that implicit in the fine control of both tone and rhythm manifested by this octave.

The most striking piece of internal (or psychological) mimesis would be, I suppose, the five stanzas of Haidée's dream (IV.31–5):

> She dreamed of being alone on the sea-shore,
>   Chained to a rock; she knew not how, but stir
> She could not from the spot, and the loud roar
>   Grew, and each wave rose roughly, threatening her;
> And o'er her upper lip they seemed to pour,
>   Until she sobbed for breath, and soon they were
> Foaming o'er her lone head, so fierce and high—
> Each broke to drown her, yet she could not die.
>
> Anon—she was released, and then she strayed
>   O'er the sharp shingles with her bleeding feet,
> And stumbled almost every step she made:
>   And something rolled before her in a sheet,
> Which she must still pursue howe'er afraid:
>   'Twas white and indistinct, nor stopped to meet
> Her glance nor grasp, for still she gazed and grasped,
> And ran, but it escaped her as she clasped.   [31–2]

The breathless quality of these long sentences (each a whole octave) is well adapted to the expression of the terror of a

7. A particularly tidy Augustan specimen of this kind of phrasal symmetry is the first stanza of Pope's "Epistle to a Young Lady on Her Leaving the Town after the Coronation."

nightmare. The smooth sequence of independent clauses loosely connected by "and" (which occurs eight times in the two octaves) suggests both the significant inconsequence of dreams in general and, in the second stanza quoted, the anxious pursuit of something that ever eludes the grasp (emphasized by the alliteration of "glance nor grasp . . . gazed and grasped") of this particular dream. The monotonous reiteration of the personal pronoun (sixteen in so many lines), on the other hand, expresses the obsession with self characteristic of the dreamer. The whole passage is restrained, economical, and thoroughly admirable.

In all the passages examined so far one is struck by the skill with which Byron manipulates such simple and conventional rhetorical devices as alliteration, assonance, consonance, internal rhyme. This is, in fact, characteristic of the poem as a whole. One is appreciative, for example, of the contempt expressed by the alliterative labials of "Power's base purveyors, who for pickings howl" (ix.27), or in the *st's* of "modern, reigning, sterling, stupid stamp!" (xii.12). Or of the suggestions of speed and monotony in the internal rhyme and alliteration of "waste, and haste, and glare, and gloss, and glitter" (x.26). Or of the further extension of the same device in the pointless briskness and orderliness in the central four lines of an octave from the Siege of Ismail:

> The troops, already disembarked, pushed on
>   To take a battery on the right: the others,
> Who landed lower down, their landing done,
>   Had set to work as briskly as their brothers:
> Being grenadiers, they mounted one by one,
>   Cheerful as children climb the breasts of mothers,
> O'er the entrenchment and the palisade,
> Quite orderly, as if upon parade.   [viii.15]

Closely related to this would be certain elementary forms of sound-imitation, such as we find in the following couplets:

When amatory poets sing their loves
  In liquid lines mellifluously bland.   [v.1]

Bombs, drums, guns, bastions, batteries, bayonets, bullets—
Hard words, which stick in the soft Muses' gullets.

[vii.78]

The liquids and nasals of the first passage are obvious enough, and Byron himself provides a gloss on the array of rhyming and alliterating vowels and mutes in the second. This last, of course, is part of the "epic" theme, and is closely related to the stanzas of cacophonous Russian names (vii.14–17). There is probably an implicit reference to the common neoclassic notion that even the commonest and most vulgar utensils took on nobility in Greek.

Byron's trick rhymes need no comment from me, and we have already had good specimens of his fondness for internal rhyme. His most effective internal rhymes, it might be noted, seem usually to be half-rhymes (assonance or consonance). Think, for example, of "Thicker than *leaves* the *lives* began to fall" (viii.9; my italics), where the consonance of the italicized words emphasizes the likeness between leaves in autumn and human lives in war. From which it is but a step to the actual repetition of the same word (my italics):

Or know who *rested* there, a foe to *rest*.   [iii.1]

  . . . risen from *death,* to be
Perchance the *death* of one she loved too well.

[iv.36]

They either *missed,* or they were never *missed,*
And added greatly to the *missing* list.   [vii.27]

In neither of the first two passages just cited is the repeated word used in quite the same sense each time, and the participle in the third passage is a rather grim pun. It is the two senses or different applications of the same word that is emphasized in such passages as the following (my italics):

> And the waves oozing through the port-hole *made*
> His berth a little damp, and him afraid.   [II.25]

> Some *take* a lover, some *take* drams or prayers,
> Some *mind* their household, others dissipation.
>   [II.201]

>   The loud tempests *raise*
> The waters, and repentance for past sinning.   [v.6]

The zeugmas in the first and third passages dramatize with admirable economy that relationship between physical cause and psychological (or spiritual) effect which is a principal motif of the poem. The same verb that indicates the objective event serves also for the subjective effect. Besides the obvious connection with the theme of the relationship between the Fall and the law of gravity, it displays another aspect of the poet's elaborately clinical objectivity in dealing with moral situations.

The second passage is interesting for its bland pairing of such apparently unlike things as lovers, drams, and prayers; or of housekeeping and dissipation. In other words, it is a form of juxtaposition, seen in its pure form in such lists as the following:

> A priest, a shark, an alderman, or pike.   [II.157]

> After long travel, Ennui, Love, or Slaughter.
>   [II.180]

> They all were heroes, conquerors, and cuckolds.
>   [II.206]

Dwarfs, dancing girls, black eunuchs, and a poet.

[III.78]

Apart from the general function of giving shape to the material, and the specific function each of these smaller devices may serve in their different contexts, they may also be of interest for their generally Augustan quality. All are staples of Augustan satire, and it was from reading the Augustans that Byron learned how to handle them. They constitute another link between Byron and the tradition of Pope.

There is little point in merely listing examples of Byron's word-play, but one might be permitted a mild protest against the condescension with which it seems often to be dismissed. The examples already cited might suggest that Byron usually knew what he was doing. And perhaps one or two not uncharacteristic specimens may profitably be invoked. First of all, consider the lines dedicated to

That monstrous hieroglyphic—that long spout
Of blood and water—*leaden* Castlereagh!

[IX.50; my italics]

These verses are part of a larger passage dealing with the familiar theme of the connection between literature and society. Here it is specifically verbal obscurity and social violence (war). After converting Castlereagh into a sphinx ("That monstrous hieroglyphic") and then into a "monstrous" combination of leviathan and drainpipe (the "spout" image is defined by the images on *both* sides of it), he concludes economically with the single attribute of "leaden"—referring at once to the *quality* of his oratory (dull, obscure, "heavy"), the *effect* of his oratory (bullets, war, death), and the *personal characteristics* that produced such oratory (his leaden stupidity; cf. VIII.10).

The second passage is from the conclusion of the famous *ubi sunt* stanzas in Canto XI:

But *"carpe diem,"* Juan, *"carpe, carpe!"*
To-morrow sees another race as gay
And transient, and devoured by the same harpy.

[xi.86]

I call attention to the use of the word "race" in the second
line. It is useful that we first think of race in terms of a race
to be run, with the suggestion of excitement and bustle and
competition (and no place to go). It is only when we come
to the third line that we find the primary reference to be to
the human race. But since the human race is seen as engaged
in a race against time, the confusion is a valuable one. This,
however, is not the only element of word-play in these
lines. Byron is joining the large number of poets who have
produced variants of the *carpe diem* theme. And he has his
own contribution. *Carpe diem,* he says, make the most of
the day, before you too are devoured by the monster death
(or time). And death is a harpy for more reasons than that it
makes possible a clever rhyme. When we recall that it was
the Harpies who snatched the food away from King Phineus
(the word "harpy" is related to *harpazô,* "to seize or snatch")
and that *carpe diem* means literally "Seize (or snatch) the
day" (*carpo* and *harpazô* are, in fact, cognates), the point of
the etymological pun becomes clear. Snatch the day, then,
before death snatches you. Or, even better, thinking of the
harpy as time: Snatch time before time snatches you. In any
case the point is clear and the device potent.

Both of the passages provide more material for analysis
than what I have called vaguely "word-play." Both, for example, are highly metaphoric, and both are specimens of
the bright, showy, self-consciously clever sort of metaphor
called conceit—a kind of image of obvious utility to a poem
in which, as we have seen, the speaker's brightness and
sophistication are of thematic importance.

We have glanced at some of the more valuable conceits in

Don Juan in the course of the previous chapters. One recalls, for example, the meteorological and physiological conceits concluding Canto II ("The heart is like the sky, etc."; 214–15), or the "frozen champagne" conceit of Canto XIII (37–8). The best known, I suppose, is the "Microcosm on stilts" passage from Canto XII (56). But these only begin to suggest the range and variety of Byron's conceits. We are given both the extended and many-faceted comparison between the coming of Suwarrow to the Russian army and a "grand illumination" in London (VII.44–6) and two lines of compressed social history (referring to the portraits at Norman Abbey):

> Steel Barons, molten the next generation
> To silken rows of gay and gartered Earls.
>
> [XIII.68]

There is the brilliant conceit of war and disease developed from a hint in the source (VIII.12) [8] and the conceit of "cities, that boil over with their scum," developed from the "dead metaphor" of a city street in "ferment" (XI.8).

But for brilliance, originality, and thematic relevance the following ranks second only to the "frozen champagne" stanzas:

> Suppose him in a handsome uniform—
>   A scarlet coat, black facings, a long plume,
> Waving, like sails new shivered in a storm,
>   Over a cocked hat in a crowded room,
> And brilliant breeches, bright as a Cairn Gorme,
>   Of yellow casimire we may presume,
> White stockings drawn uncurdled as new milk
> O'er limbs whose symmetry set off the silk;
>
> Suppose him sword by side, and hat in hand,
>   Made up by Youth, Fame, and an army tailor—

---

8. *Poetry, 6,* 334 n. 2.

> That great enchanter, at whose rod's command
>   Beauty springs forth, and Nature's self turns paler,
> Seeing how Art can make her work more grand
>   (When she don't pin men's limbs in like a gaoler),—
> Behold him placed as if upon a pillar! He
> Seems Love turned a Lieutenant of Artillery!
>
> His bandage slipped down into a cravat—
>   His wings subdued to epaulettes—his quiver
> Shrunk to a scabbard, with his arrows at
>   His side as a small sword, but sharp as ever—
> His brow converted into a cocked hat—
>   But still so like, that Psyche were more clever
> Than some wives (who make blunders no less stupid),
> If she had not mistaken him for Cupid.   [IX.43–5]

Coming as it does at the very beginning of Juan's adventure with Catherine the Great, this passage occupies a particularly crucial position in the development of the action. For, as Steffan has observed, the affair with Catherine is for Juan an initiation in a sense in which none of his previous affairs had been.[9] In spite of everything, Byron manages to make us accept the idea of Juan's "innocence" (in the special sense of the word used in this essay). But after his excursions in Petersburg this is no longer possible. But then, it is no longer the effect Byron wants to produce. Catherine is, in the first place, an "older woman." She is described, I have suggested, in terms of a kind of travesty of the "stern sweetness" paradox. She is an empress, an embodiment of absolute secular power (a tyrant). She is lustful and she is given to waging war. She possesses great wealth.

9. *Variorum, 1,* 284. It is worth noticing that this is the point in the poem where Juan comes in contact with the little Turkish orphan, Leila As Rupert Palmer has called to my attention, the little girl now serves to replace Juan as the embodiment of what I have been calling "innocence." In so doing she can serve as a means of gauging the extent of Juan's departure from this state.

She is, in fact, like Lambro, an almost definitive expression of "experience"—*from one point of view*. When Juan enters her arms, he is entering an entirely new phase of existence. The attitude is, of course, a double one, but at least with regard to Catherine herself the judgment is predominantly adverse. It is only with Adeline (so very different and so very like) and (in still another way) Aurora that the weight shifts distinctly toward the other pole. But at no time is Byron unaware of what is involved, as these three splendid octaves make clear.

This is, as I see it, one of those passages that occur from time to time in which a number of central issues dealt with throughout the poem are brought together and given a firmer and more authoritative statement than is possible in the more diffuse, discursive mode of the poem as a whole. They are of greatest value, perhaps, in the sharper definition of relationships which they make possible. The importance of such centers of meaning in so long and so deliberately casual a poem is obvious.[1] This is especially the case when we recall that Byron (like Spenser in the Bowre of Blisse) normally works by building up and tearing down his values, relating them by juxtaposition and by means of plot, *persona,* and structural metaphor. It is only at certain points (such as the passage just quoted) that we have the kind of irony we have been instructed to admire. But these centers merely affirm what is implicit throughout.

Here, then, on the threshold of Juan's definitive initiation into the world of experience, we are given a passage that not only reminds us of much of what is involved in this initiation, but, much more important, looks beyond the affair with Catherine to kinds of value that can emerge only later (that is, in the English cantos). We have here a

1. Byron's use of this device is one of the most interesting stylistic analogies between *Don Juan* and *Childe Harold.*

particularly effective rehearsal of the art-nature motif presented by the description of the hero as a military Eros: "Love turned a Lieutenant of Artillery." Even this particularly repellent manifestation of the world of experience is at least susceptible of aesthetic exploitation—by a good tailor, say, or a poet. The conceit itself is a remarkably resonant one, with its reminiscence of the blind god who arouses irrational passions, often maliciously, through the wounds made by his arrows (Juan has changed roles from I.88; he is now the wounder rather than the wounded). The effect is achieved, it will be noted, by combining the two cupids, the mischievous little god with the bow and arrows and the beautiful youth of the Cupid and Psyche legend.

With the discussion of this group of three stanzas we have moved beyond the smaller elements with which we have been for the most part concerned to the larger structural units. Now the centrifugal pressure in a poem like *Don Juan* is clearly enormous. And just as one may feel that a tension between push and resistance is one of the most exciting qualities of Byron's handling of rhythm, much of the peculiar effect of the poem as a whole is a function of the interaction of forces pushing us onward and forces compelling us to linger. There are all kinds of interesting possibilities. An element (e.g. a digression) that may be retarding with reference to a larger unit (e.g. a particular episode) will have an opposite effect with regard to smaller retarding elements within itself. Byron is ingenious in devising ways of inducing the reader not to move through the poem too quickly. Rhythm, rhyme, formal rhetorical patterning, as we have seen, all have a part to play in the creation of this singularly fruitful tension between octave and the conversational flow.

But if Byron shows admirable inventiveness in investing his octaves with sufficient interest to keep them from getting lost in the conversational rush, he is perhaps not uniformly successful in his control of the rush itself. While there is no lack of substance in *Don Juan*, there is sometimes lack of direction. Some of this, of course, is good, in that it serves to make us pause and wonder about the function of any one particular element. But sometimes it is merely clumsy.

Byron was not unaware of the problem. Indeed, one of the most effective ways of dealing with it is one he inherited from his Italian models—to disarm us by calling attention to the difficulty. The device has the further advantage, from one point of view, of dramatizing the difference in style and technique between *Don Juan* and the "other epics":

> I feel this tediousness will never do—
> 'Tis being *too* epic.   [III.111]

Another useful method of sharpening the direction of the stanzas is displayed in the extended conceit examined above. It is the simple rhetorical device of repeating the (usually) first phrase of (usually) successive octaves (here "Suppose him," "Suppose him"):

> It was upon a day, a summer's day . . .
> 'Twas on a summer's day—the sixth of June . . .
> 'Twas on the sixth of June . . .   [I.102, 103, 104]

> So Juan stood . . .
> Don Juan stood . . .   [II.13, 14]

> So Juan wept . . .
> And Juan wept . . .   [II.16, 17]

> Oh, thou eternal Homer!
> Oh, thou eternal Homer!   [VII.79, 80]

> He was a bachelor . . .
> But Juan was a bachelor . . .   [XI.46, 47]

But no amount of merely rhetorical organization, after all, or even of accomplished manipulation of individual image and individual unit of meaning can confer real structural (as opposed to merely thematic) unity on a poem. They themselves derive their significance from their participation in the ruling structural principles. The greater part of this study has been concerned with analysis of three of these: the metaphor of the fall, the use of the *persona,* and the idea of epic satire. The development of these three patterns may be thought of as constituting the proper plot of *Don Juan.* It is in terms of them that Juan's personal development from his boy-love of Julia through the testing on the sea, the edenic relationship with Haidée, the more sophisticated transitional adventures in Constantinople, the morally compromising experiences at Ismail and Moscow, and the urbane doings in London and Norman Abbey (that is, the movement from innocence to experience) is dramatized, defined, made humanly relevant. For if the poem is unified, it is not static. The same points are made again and again, presented in (and tested by) different contexts, elaborated and sophisticated. Along with the exposition and elaboration of motif we have not merely the movement of the narrative plot, but also that much more central plot movement which may most clearly be conceived in terms of the altering relationship between speaker and protagonist. And all these plots and devices lead to and are constantly involved in the delicate expression of a highly individual attitude— that is, the *tone* of *Don Juan.*

Though I have not made a point of it, I have throughout this study been concerned with what are ultimately tonal problems. While matters of tone are of obvious importance in any literary work, I think it may fairly be argued that they are peculiarly crucial to Byron's poem. There is a sense, after all, in which we may properly agree with Arnold's prim judgment on the author of *Don Juan,* that he teaches us little. *Don Juan* is not a poem of content; it is a poem of reaction—and it is the reaction which, in the sense of "meaning," is the content. It is less the world view as such than the way it is taken.

Another comparison may help to dramatize this special importance of tone in *Don Juan*, and contribute to our understanding of the sense in which Byron is and is not in the tradition of the eighteenth century. Fielding's *Tom Jones* is a book Byron knew well and with which, as with the picaresque tradition in general, Byron's poem has evident connection. At the beginning of Bk. i, chapter 4, Fielding gives us an extended description of Paradise Hall, the seat of Squire Allworthy. He is mostly interested in the landscape, dismissing the house itself, the villages, and the ruined abbey in only a few lines. The landscape is varied but uniform. Agreeably to the aesthetic bias of the work as a whole (which is a moral bias as well), Fielding emphasizes the fact that it all owes "less to art than to Nature." There is a romantic ruin off in the distance, with some "wild mountains" rounding off the view. While I do not at all suppose that anything of the sort was designed, it is clear that the description bears a more than vaguely symbolic relation to the whole work. Fielding, in his desire to present a comprehensive view of human nature, has to take account of the strong element of the irrational and adventitious in even the least eccentric human experience. He provides us with dark passions (it is striking how often the word "hate" and its synonyms occur in the book), and few readers have missed the role played by Fortune and coincidence in the economy of the novel. But the dark passions are like the wild mountains: they are not felt as central, and they are ultimately apprehended as part of a moral and aesthetic pattern which is reassuringly harmonious; while Fortune and coincidence ultimately build up an elaborate but completely analyzable structure in terms of which every element of the plot is in some sense accounted for and justified.[2] It is in effect a kind of rationalized version of Milton's vision of an all-encompassing providential order in *Paradise Lost*.

I have spoken of the necessity of considering the poet of *Don Juan* as in an important sense a rationalist in the eighteenth-century tradition. But there are differences. In the thirteenth canto of *Don Juan* Byron gives us his own version of an English estate, Norman Abbey, the country seat of the Amundevilles. Norman Abbey is the local embodiment of much of Byron's point of view. It is a great house and a ruin, a place where the relation between man and the forces of time has been worked out in an especially definitive manner. To put it crudely, time has destroyed and conferred charm. The paradox is a romantic commonplace, but it takes on new life from its context, its participation in the tryingly paradoxical but endurable (and much more than endurable) world of *Don Juan*. Norman Abbey has strong social implications. It is the setting for and an expression of those social values which Byron is engaged in developing. The family portraits in the gallery, for example, express both the ominous and the charming aspects of life in society. And elements of the nature description are at least susceptible to a kind of explicit allegorization foreign to Fielding:

> Before the mansion lay a lucid Lake,
>> Broad as transparent, deep, and freshly fed
> By a river, which its softened way did take
>> In currents through the calmer water spread
> Around: the wildfowl nestled in the brake
>> And sedges, brooding in their liquid bed:
> The woods sloped downwards to its brink, and stood
> With their green faces fixed upon the flood.

2. My comments on *Tom Jones* are indebted to the discussion in Dorothy Van Ghent's *The English Novel. Form and Function* (New York, Rinehart, 1955), pp. 65–81.

Its outlet dashed into a deep cascade,
　Sparkling with foam, until again subsiding,
Its shriller echoes—like an infant made
　Quiet—sank into softer ripples, gliding
Into a rivulet; and thus allayed,
　Pursued its course, now gleaming and now hiding
Its windings through the woods; now clear, now blue,
According as the skies their shadows threw.

[XIII.57–8]

After a delightful, "natural" prenatal existence, let us say, the spirit (and at least tentative association of spirit and running water cannot be merely arbitrary) descends with some violence into a world where—"like an infant made / Quiet"—it makes itself at home, and runs off into a rivulet that pursues a winding and uncertain course (cf. the wanderings of Juan), sensitively responsive to stimuli from without (it is *mobile*). The point-by-point application to *Don Juan,* or the possibility of it, should require no comment. I do not insist upon any of this, but the possibility of allegory here is interesting to contemplate. A good though inexact analogy would be Yeats' "Coole and Ballylee."

Now this is, to say the least, rather more problematic than anything Fielding essays in *Tom Jones;* [3] for if Fielding gives us implicitly a rationalized version of Miltonic providence, Byron most explicitly uses a secularized version of the myth of the Fall as his basic organizing principle. No less than Fielding, Byron believes that human reason may profitably be applied to human experience. Far from constituting an exception to this generalization, the English cantos are clearly the poem's fullest statement of an essentially Augustan reasonableness. A characteristic quality of eighteenth-century literary rationalism, after all, was the

---

3. By "this" I mean the kind of structure that makes allegory of this kind possible, or even invites it.

extreme modesty of its claims. So far as I can see, the whole of Don Juan exists in a universe that functions in terms of certain apparently immutable and rationally intelligible laws. The difficulty arises only when one realizes that the processes defined by these laws are paradoxical.

Byron is caught and he knows he is caught and he must manage to live in terms of this awareness. This is what he is engaged in coming to terms with, and *Don Juan* is the final expression of the *quality* of this acquiescence. It is clearly a frightening vision, and Byron does not try to minimize the terror. In *Don Juan* at any rate, he wastes little time in feeling sorry either for himself or us. If he has no real answers, the firmness with which he poses the question is not contemptible, and the poise with which he manages, for the most part, to keep his fragmentary world from breaking up completely is really astonishing. For it is ultimately up to him. It is his attitude alone than can give it what coherence it is susceptible of. That is, I suppose, why he sometimes attitudinizes.

I should not care to deny that *Don Juan* is an uneven work and that the balance attained with such difficulty does not sometimes wobble dangerously. Such passages as the reference to King David's "blister" (1.168) are painful enough. Many other passages, however, have disturbed intelligent and sympathetic readers largely because of an excessively narrow frame of reference. A notorious example of Byron's alleged tonal irresponsibility would be the straight pathos of the episode of the two fathers and two sons interjected into the predominantly sardonic shipwreck scene:

> There were two fathers in this ghastly crew,
>   And with them their two sons, of whom the one
> Was more robust and hardy to the view,
>   But he died early; and when he was gone,
> His nearest messmate told his sire, who threw

One glance at him, and said, "Heaven's will be done!
I can do nothing," and he saw him thrown
Into the deep without a tear or groan.

The other father had a weaklier child,
    Of a soft cheek, and aspect delicate;
But the boy bore up long, and with a mild
    And patient spirit held aloof his fate;
Little he said, and now and then he smiled,
    As if to win a part from off the weight
He saw increasing on his father's heart,
With the deep deadly thought, that they must part.

And o'er him bent his sire, and never raised
    His eyes from off his face, but wiped the foam
From his pale lips, and ever on him gazed,
    And when the wished-for shower at length was come,
And the boy's eyes, which the dull film half glazed,
    Brightened, and for a moment seemed to roam,
He squeezed from out a rag some drops of rain
Into his dying child's mouth—but in vain.

The boy expired—the father held the clay,
    And looked upon it long, and when at last
Death left no doubt, and the dead burthen lay
    Stiff on his heart, and pulse and hope were past,
He watched it wistfully, until away
    'Twas borne by the rude wave wherein 'twas cast;
Then he himself sunk down all dumb and shivering,
And gave no sign of life, save his limbs quivering.

[II.87–90]

I do not think this Byron at his best, but it may be helpful
to see that the passage is by no means mere emotional expediency. In the preceding stanza (II.86) Byron has spoken
wryly of what seems to him the callousness of the orthodox
Christian view of eternal damnation. The Christian accepts

the notion of a hell, of course, not because he is charmed by the idea in itself but because he sees it as an intelligible part of a divine plan which is ultimately coherent and beneficent. The world of *Don Juan,* however, possesses no such intelligibility. In this it differs from both *Paradise Lost* and *Tom Jones,* taken as embodiments of worlds of grace and of reason.

The point of the shipwreck is that it is pointless. And it is this pointlessness that Byron's apparently heartless humor is calculated to dramatize. Happenings such as this, the poet suggests, make Milton's notion of a providential order seem silly. The whole of the second canto, it should be noted, is especially rich in mocking allusions to the idea of Providence. There are, for example, the repeated references to Noah's ark (II.8, 65, 95, and, implicitly, 91–2). The rainbow seen by the dying men is especially effective. They thought it a good omen; but they learned better. And again Byron indicates value by emphasizing the gaudiness of the rainbow. Or, a bit later, if one has *Paradise Lost* in mind in connection with Byron's island Eden, it is not hard to see in Lambro confronting the errant Juan and Haidée an allusion to Milton's Christ judging a sinful Adam and Eve.[4] The only moral order Byron can perceive is related to that hard world of time and disillusion which is the version of experience presented in the early part of the poem.

But if one way of undermining the traditional notion of Providence (in order to make way for his own version) is by making it seem silly, another is to emphasize what seems to the poet its essential inhumanity. The poet cannot be merely light-hearted when it is suggested, as the first father suggests after the death of his son, that it is all "Heaven's will." It is like his indignation when Wordsworth proclaims that Carnage is "God's daughter" (VIII.9). What he wants to do here is, quite existentially, to bring home to us the terri-

4. My students called this to my attention.

ble human suffering that may be concealed by the formula "Heaven's will be done," or by any attempt easily to assert an abstract order for which the poet is unable to detect much concrete evidence. If the error lies in the inadequacy of the poet's vision, one cannot complain of the adequacy with which that vision is presented.

Milton's assertion of Eternal Providence, it will be recalled, is explicitly associated with the epic style. The epic style is the high style, and its height not only is appropriate to the dignity of the content but is an integral part of the vision. Providence needs to be asserted, Milton says, because man's vision is limited, and his poem is an attempt imaginatively to enable man to see through the eyes of God. One must ascend in order to perceive the pattern in terms of which the Fall is fortunate. But this is an ascent that can be made only in faith (it is technically the gift of Wisdom), which means it is an ascent that Byron cannot make— though one gets the impression that he wishes he could. Fielding had lost the world of grace, but had managed to retain the world of reason. For Byron this too has largely slipped away, and the only significance to be asserted is that of a unique response to a world one does not understand. Byron's response is secular and social, and its artistic expression is the plain manner of satire and conversation. But because it is an attempt at finding matter for assertion, it may claim to be epic. From the poet's point of view, at least, his is an "argument /Not less but more Heroic" than that of the classical epics, or even Milton's. In any case, it is a great deal more desperate.

I should hold then that, if taken seriously, *Don Juan* is not an entirely comfortable poem. And to take it seriously is not to forget or even minimize the comic (though my own purposes in this study have prescribed a certain sobriety). It is fun and life is fun and that is an important part of the point. For the last word is gracious:

But Heaven must be diverted; its diversion
Is sometimes truculent—but never mind:
The World upon the whole is worth the assertion
(If but for comfort) that all things are kind.

[XIII.41]

If Milton, therefore, in the Vallombrosa passage of *Paradise Lost* (Bk. I, ll. 301–4), can dramatize his vision of an ultimately beneficent divine purpose by presenting Hell itself in terms of a scene of extraordinary loveliness, Byron may dramatize his own secular and social coming to terms with reality through the laughter of a gentleman. And just as the high style of Milton's celestial Muse is answerable to Milton's heroic and religious vision, so the style of Byron's "pedestrian Muses" has, in its very different way, become a world view and a way of life.

Appendix A

"EPIC" AND "ROMAUNT"

IN THE COURSE of the foregoing discussion I have had more than one occasion to refer to *Childe Harold,* suggesting in particular the relevance of comparing the use of the Prometheus myth in *Childe Harold* with the use of the myth of the Fall in *Don Juan.* Other equally significant points of contact have been glanced at. There is a sense in which *Childe Harold* is an earlier and more characteristically romantic attempt at making a statement in some ways remarkably similar to the statement I have been trying to define in the later poem. I do not mean I think it merely a groping attempt to say something *Don Juan* says better. There are qualities of the statement of *Childe Harold* for which *Don Juan,* for all its greater range and control, provides no adequate equivalent. I learned to read *Don Juan* by reading *Childe Harold,* and the present study is in large part an application to the later poem of principles first educed from the earlier. It is not only that the theme of both works is analogous; the same formal organizing devices are present in both.

To take the least important point first, one is inevitably reminded in reading *Don Juan* of the curious relation between speaker and protagonist in the earlier poem; for if the hero of *Don Juan* seems sometimes rather bland, the protagonist of *Childe Harold* is, as a character, nonexistent. In his preface to the first two cantos Byron himself dismisses him as a "fictitious character . . . introduced for the sake of giving some connection to the piece." And in the last two cantos he hardly appears at all. He does, however, serve to focus and, to some extent, to dramatize certain aspects of the character of the speaker himself in a way that might be felt as dimly foreshadowing the later and more sophisticated techniques of *Don Juan*.

There are other points of contact of much greater value. As I read it, one of the most striking qualities of Byron's *Don Juan* is the use of aesthetic theory (specifically, the doctrine of the styles) as a structural device. And to this *Childe Harold*, in its very different way, presents some remarkable analogies.

The third and fourth cantos of *Childe Harold* (which may properly, from one point of view, be considered as in themselves a complete poem) [1] are constructed in terms of a curious and highly personal combination of two very different aesthetic traditions, the romantic and the neoclassic. The third canto, indeed, begins with a consideration of the nature and function of artistic creation, especially as applied to the present poem. It is described as specifically compensative. The artist, by virtue of his superior sensibility, is inevitably alienated from ordinary satisfactions. But by virtue of his imaginative power he can create an ideal world and ideal companions which not only make up for but in a sense are more real than the world and the humanity that he feels has let him down:

1. Cf. H. J. C. Grierson, ed., *Poems of Lord Byron* (London, Chatto & Windus, 1923), p. ix: "The last two cantos of *Childe Harold* are a single and unique poem. They have the slightest connection with the previous cantos." See also Roy Fuller, ed., *Byron for Today* (London, Porcupine Press, 1948), p. 13: "With all their faults, these two cantos obviously constitute a great poem."

He, who grown agèd in this world of woe,
  In deeds, not years, piercing the depths of life,
  So that no wonder waits him—nor below
  Can Love or Sorrow, Fame, Ambition, Strife,
  Cut to his heart again with the keen knife
  Of silent, sharp endurance—he can tell
  Why Thought seeks refuge in lone caves, yet rife
  With airy images, and shapes which dwell
Still unimpaired, though old, in the Soul's haunted cell.

'Tis to create, and in creating live
  A being more intense that we endow
  With form our fancy, gaining as we give
  The life we image, *even as I do now*—
  What am I? Nothing: but not so art thou,
  Soul of my thought! with whom I traverse earth,
  Invisible but gazing, as I glow
  Mixed with thy spirit, blended with thy birth,
And feeling still with thee in my crushed feelings' dearth.
                              [III.5–6; my italics]

    The *locus classicus* of this sort of thing is, I gather, those
pages of the *Confessions* (Bk. IX) in which Rousseau speaks
of how he satisfied through imaginative creation that "desire
of loving, which I had never been able to satisfy, and by
which I felt myself devoured." [2] The result was the *Nouvelle Héloïse*, which Byron had been reading during the
composition of *Childe Harold*, III. [3]
    The situation for Byron is a little more complex. He is
already aware of that paradoxical relationship between disease and remedy we have been observing in *Don Juan*.
"Thought," which for Byron is as much an imaginative
and emotional as an intellectual activity (cf. the Petrarchan

    2. *The Confessions of Jean Jacques Rousseau* (New York, Modern Library,
n.d.), pp. 440–6.
    3. See, for example, *LJ, 3,* 335 (June 27, 1816).

pensier), and which seeks peace in imaginative creation, may actually find its maladies increased:

> Yet must I think less wildly:—I *have* thought
>   Too long and darkly, till my brain became,
>   In its own eddy boiling and o'erwrought,
>   A whirling gulf of phantasy and flame:
>   And thus, untaught in youth my heart to tame,
>   My springs of life were poisoned. 'Tis too late!
>   Yet am I changed; though still enough the same
>   In strength to bear what Time can not abate,
> And feed on bitter fruits without accusing Fate.
>
> [III.7]

And so, still in terms of the concept of imaginative compensation, the poet turns to the figure of a resigned and stoic Harold:

> Self-exiled Harold wanders forth again,
>   With nought of Hope left—but with less of gloom;
>   The very knowledge that he lived in vain,
>   That all was over on this side the tomb,
>   Had made Despair a smilingness assume,
>   Which, though 'twere wild,—as on the plundered wreck
>   When mariners would madly meet their doom
>   With draughts intemperate on the sinking deck,—
> Did yet inspire a cheer, which he forebore to check.
>
> [III.16]

In the composition of the *Nouvelle Héloïse* Rousseau had sought relief by identifying himself with the lover, Saint-Preux. Through Harold, Byron hopes to find, if not peace, at least diversion and a means of channeling his own unruly passions:

> Yet, though a dreary strain, to this I cling;
>   So that it wean me from the weary dream

Of selfish grief or gladness—so it fling
Forgetfulness around me—it shall seem
To me, though to none else, a not ungrateful theme.

[4]

Thus a distinctive rendering of the Rousseauist concept of imaginative compensation supplies the poet with a means of dramatizing the difficulties and possibilities of his own situation ("even as I do now").

But Rousseauist reverie is not the only solution whose implications are explored through the poem (it should be clear even from the few stanzas quoted that this form of compensation will not ultimately be satisfactory). Or rather, it unites to form a curious hybrid with neoclassic aesthetic theory,[4] which itself implies a philosophy of life, peculiarly relevant to one whose problem is, in part, the government of the passions (cf. *Don Juan*).

The point of view perhaps receives its best statement in the lines on the Apollo Belvidere:

Or view the Lord of the unerring bow,
  The God of Life, and Poesy, and Light—
  The Sun in human limbs arrayed, and brow
  All radiant from his triumph in the fight;
  The shaft hath just been shot—the arrow bright
  With an Immortal's vengeance—in his eye
  And nostril beautiful Disdain, and Might
  And Majesty, flash their full lightnings by,
Developing in that one glance the Deity.

But in his delicate form—a dream of Love,
  Shaped by some solitary Nymph, whose breast
  Longed for a deathless lover from above,
  And maddened in that vision—are exprest

4. Cf. Stephen A. Larrabee, *English Bards and Grecian Marbles. The Relationship between Sculpture and Poetry, Especially in the Romantic Period* (New York, Columbia Univ. Press, 1943), pp. 158–74.

> All that ideal Beauty ever blessed
> The mind with in its most unearthly mood,
> When each Conception was a heavenly Guest—
> A ray of Immortality—and stood,
> Starlike, around, until they gathered to a God!
>
> [IV.161–2]

In the second stanza we have a variant of the persistent theme of art as the ideal embodiment of personal aspiration. But it is the first stanza with which at the moment I am more concerned. The important thing here, for our immediate purpose, is the emphasis on the specifically neoclassic ideal of the frozen moment, the significant gesture—"The shaft hath just been shot, etc." The same motif is found in the stanza on the Laocoön (IV.160) or the Dying Gladiator (IV.140). And in both of these latter instances the gesture is one of "torture dignifying pain," suffering ennobled by the manner in which it is accepted. A valuable complication of the theme is found in the stanza on the death of Caesar (IV.87). Caesar dies at the foot of Pompey's statue: but it is the dying man himself who is "statuesque"—"Folding his robe in dying dignity." His graceful acceptance of death parallels Sulla's laying down "With an atoning smile a more than earthly crown" (IV.83), and is in strong contrast to the "bastard Cæsar," Napoleon (IV.90), who is unable to bend gracefully to adversity. It is this motif that gives force to the final almost gay gesture of acceptance of the vehicle of exile (to be contrasted with the equivocal attitude of III.1–2). For it is in the act of pilgrimage itself that the pilgrim professes to find the value he is seeking:

> And I have loved thee, Ocean! and my joy
> Of youthful sports was on thy breast to be
> Borne, like thy bubbles, onward: from a boy
> I wantoned with thy breakers—they to me

Were a delight; and if the freshening sea
Made them a terror—'twas a pleasing fear,
For I was as it were a Child of thee,
And trusted to thy billows far and near,
And laid my hand upon thy mane—*as I do here*.

[IV.184; my italics]

The poet himself can now make the heroic gesture. And the "as I do here" of this passage should be compared with the "as I do now" of the earlier one.

Both poems, then, from one point of view, are enactments of a coming to terms with life (or the world of "experience," to employ the term I have been using in this study). But the acceptance is not simple or simply won.

I submit that unless one is alive to what the poet is doing with aesthetic theory (in itself, perhaps, of no particular interest), he would be missing a good deal of the point of *Childe Harold*. The Rousseauist and neoclassic aesthetics are used as dramatic devices in the poet's enactment of a knightly adventure. These unifying elements are included within a larger frame which, in its vaguer and more haphazard way, is distinctly suggestive of *Don Juan*. For if Juan is protagonist in a particular reworking of the epic tradition, Harold is the ostensible hero of a poem which Byron has chosen to call a "romaunt." That he really means what he seems to mean by this designation is suggested by his vigorous defense of Harold's "chivalric" qualities in the "addition" to the preface to the first two cantos.[5] But it is clear enough from the poem itself. The tradition is that of

5. The third and fourth cantos, to be sure, were not styled "romaunt" in their separate editions. But the conception of romaunt is surely part of that "theme" which the poet "seizes" again in III.3. When the four cantos were collected in 1819, the whole work was again given the subtitle "A Romaunt." Cf. the reference to the *"Romaunts* of Masters Cottle, Laureat Pye, Ogilvy, Hole, and gentle Mistress Cowley," which "have not exalted the Epic Muse" (*English Bards*, note to l. 225; my italics).

the romance-epic—of Spenser and the Italians—and Byron expects us to bear that in mind as we follow him in his radical recasting of the traditional mode.

That Byron, at the time he wrote *Childe Harold,* had any very profound knowledge of either Spenser or his Italian models is, I suppose, doubtful. But he had the general idea, and that is all we need. The title, use of the Spenserian stanza, archaisms, and introduction of specifically chivalric terms and concepts make the intention clear enough. We are dealing with a knight who is to have adventures in the course of some sort of pilgrimage—and the whole is to be richly endowed with moral implications:

> Onward he flies, nor fixed as yet the goal
> Where he shall rest him on his pilgrimage;
> And o'er him many changing scenes must roll
> Ere toil his thirst for travel can assuage,
> Or he shall calm his breast, or learn experience sage.
>
> [1.28]

> Farewell, with *him* alone may rest the pain,
> If such there were—with *you* the Moral of his Strain.
>
> [IV.186]

Speaking of what he calls the "low mimetic" mode characteristic of the Romantic period, Northrop Frye has observed: "The encyclopaedic tendency of this period is toward the construction of mythological epics in which the myths represent psychological or subjective states of mind." [6] This is not too unlike what we find in *Childe Harold. Childe Harold* is clearly a subjective version of the romance, a transformation of the perils and rewards of the knight errant into the search for value on the part of a single alienated individual. The Pilgrim faces up to one after another of the traditional *loci* of value of Western culture, engages

---

6. *Anatomy of Criticism* (Princeton Univ. Press, 1957), p. 60.

himself imaginatively with them, seeking always to find a value in pilgrimage to replace that forfeited by exile. The romance form not only dramatizes the daring and dignity and generally human relevance of the action, but at the same time makes possible the sense of loss that one feels when one compares Childe Harold's self-conscious fumbling with the world of traditional romance—which, if filled with dangers, was also a world in which right triumphed and the value sought was to be obtained. Childe Harold obtains a value, to be sure. But it is a good deal less restful than what he was looking for.

Appendix B

MOBILITY AND IMPROVISATION

IN TWO FAMOUS STANZAS Byron endows the Lady Adeline with a quality he calls "mobility":

> So well she acted all and every part
>   By turns—with that vivacious versatility,
> Which many people take for want of heart.
>   They err—'tis merely what is called mobility,
> A thing of temperament and not of art,
>   Though seeming so, from its supposed facility;
> And false—though true; for, surely, they're sincerest
> Who are strongly acted on by what is nearest.
>
> This makes your actors, artists, and romancers,
>   Heroes sometimes, though seldom—sages never:
> But speakers, bards, diplomatists, and dancers,
>   Little that's great, but much of what is clever;
> Most orators, but very few financiers,
>   Though all Exchequer Chancellors endeavour
> Of late years, to dispense with Cocker's rigours,
> And grow quite figurative with their figures.
>
> [XVI.97–8]

There is no need to dwell on the tonal refinement of these octaves. It is clear enough that Byron is both asserting a value and suggesting its dangers. And the value asserted is one clearly relevant to the sophistication he is in process of defining. But I do want to call attention to a likely source for Byron's notion of what, according to his note, is called

> in French *"mobilité."* I am not sure that mobility is English; but it is expressive of a quality which rather belongs to other climates, though it is sometimes seen to a great extent in our own. It may be defined as an excessive susceptibility of immediate impressions—at the same time without *losing* the past: and is, though sometimes apparently useful to the possessor, a most painful and unhappy attribute.[1]

It will be noticed that Byron is uneasy about the word. Not only is it not a naturalized English word, but the quality it stands for is at least not characteristically British. It is associated with "other climates," presumably warmer ones.

There is ample evidence of Byron's acquaintance with the novel *Corinne,* by Mme. de Staël, whom he had known in London in 1813 and in Switzerland in 1816. E. H. Coleridge, for example, has pointed out that *Corinne* supplies a model for the description of the Coliseum by moonlight in *Childe Harold,* IV.[2] John Churton Collins, in his review of the Coleridge-Prothero edition of the *Works,* has suggested that Byron drew on *Corinne* in the apostrophe to Ocean in the same poem, as well as for the character of the Childe.[3] It may be worth pointing out, then, that in Mme. de Staël's novel *mobilité* is clearly associated with Latin Europe, and especially with Corinne herself.

The following is characteristic. On Holy Thursday the hero, Oswald, Lord Nelvil, meets Corinne at the Vatican after a separation of several days. When Corinne first sees Oswald, she trembles so that "in order to go on, she had to

1. *Poetry,* 6, 600–1 n. 1.
2. *Ibid.,* 2, 424 n. 1.
3. "The Works of Lord Byron," *Quarterly Review,* 202 (1905), 438.

support herself on the balustrade. At that moment the *Miserere* began." The music and the surroundings draw Corinne's attention from all earthly things. "Even Oswald became invisible to her." As long as the liturgy continues, Corinne remains in her state of religious exaltation. But her shift in mood is again abrupt:

> When she had finished her devotions, she arose. Lord Nelvil did not yet dare approach her, out of respect for the religious meditation in which he believed her immersed. But she came to him herself in a transport of happiness. And, with this sentiment expanding over everything she did, she greeted gayly and vivaciously those whom she met in a Saint Peter's now suddenly become a great public promenade, a place of rendezvous for the discussion of business and pleasure.
>
> Oswald was astonished by this mobility which permitted such radically different impressions to follow each other so closely.[4]

Oswald was astonished as Juan was astonished, wondering "how much of Adeline was *real*" (xvi.96). And in neither case, as both authors make clear, is the censure implied in the astonishment to be taken as normative. Adeline's mobility is another version of that growing urbanity Byron has so praised in his hero himself: "The art of living in all climes with ease" (xv.11), while the *mobilité* of Corinne is essential both to her charm as a woman and her power as an artist.

From the viewpoint of Byron's hero it is the personal value (with its appropriate qualifications) that matters most. But with regard to the *persona* it is of course the artistic implications that must be considered. Now one of the most frequent generalizations about Byron's manner, especially

4. *Corinne, ou l'Italie* (Paris, Garnier Frères, n.d.), pp. 197-8 (Bk. x, ch. 4). My translation.

in the long poems, is that it is improvisational. The most intelligent development of this notion is probably that in a fine essay by Sir Herbert Grierson, where we read of Byron's "strain of passionate improvisation." [5] And Byron himself has given it sanction in two stanzas of *Don Juan:*

> I perch upon an humbler promontory,
>   Amidst Life's infinite variety:
> With no great care for what is nicknamed Glory,
>   But speculating as I cast mine eye
> On what may suit or may not suit my story,
>   And never straining hard to versify,
> I rattle on exactly as I'd talk
> With anybody in a ride or walk.
>
> I don't know that there may be much ability
>   Shown in this sort of desultory rhyme;
> But there's a conversational facility,
>   Which may round off an hour upon a time.
> Of this I'm sure at least, there's no servility
>   In mine irregularity of chime,
> Which rings what's uppermost of new or hoary,
> Just as I feel the *Improvvisatore.*   [xv.19–20]

The first point to be noticed is the evident likeness between the faculty Byron calls mobility and what he is here associating with "the *Improvvisatore.*" And we are again reminded of the persistent relation between hero and *persona.* The second is the fact that not only *mobilité* but improvisation has an important part to play in *Corinne;* for the *mobile* Corinne is by vocation an *improvvisatrice.* Furthermore, according to Geneviève Gennari, the very concept of improvisation as understood in the early nineteenth century was largely the creation of Mme. de Staël:

5. "Lord Byron: Arnold and Swinburne," *The Background of English Literature* (London, Chatto and Windus, 1925), p. 84.

It was . . . she who gave immortality to the genre. Without her it would have been long since forgotten. . . . It is in vain that she warns us that *the improvisation of Corinne differs completely from anything the Italians call by that name.* One of the titles of which Corinne remains most assured is precisely that of improvvisatrice. She, by the mere prestige of her name, gave new dignity to a genre generally despised.[6]

This, if true, is important. And it is certainly most unlikely that there is much point in referring us, as does Pratt, to "the famous Sgricci," who seems never to have been an extemporizer in the "conversational" sense required by Byron's description (as Pratt observes, he improvised tragedies).[7] Nor have I found any likely precedents in the only detailed discussion of improvisation I have come across.[8] Corinne, on the other hand, describes her art as follows:

I consider improvisation as *a kind of animated conversation.* I do not permit myself to be tied down to any particular subject. I abandon myself to the impression which the interest of my audience produces on me, and it is to my friends that I owe the greater part of my ability in this mode.[9]

I think there is a chance, therefore, that this enormously popular novel by Mme. de Staël made a contribution to Byron's *Don Juan,* helping him define both the kind of value that develops in the course of the poem and the nature of the developing relationship between hero and *persona.*

6. Geneviève Gennari, *Le Premier Voyage de Madame de Staël en Italie et la Genèse de Corinne* (Paris, Boivin, 1947), pp. 137–8. My translation, my italics.

7. *Variorum, 4,* 270.

8. Adele Vitagliano, *Storia della poesia estemporanea nella letteratura Italiana dalle origini ai nostri giorni,* Rome, Ermanno Loescher, 1905.

9. *Corinne,* pp. 48–9 (Bk. III, ch. 3). My translation, my italics. I am not aware that it has been pointed out that the specimens of Corinne's improvisation given to us in the novel are very suggestive of the mode of *Childe Harold,* especially in the last two cantos.

INDEX

Only the names of persons important to the design of the book are listed. All characters, and persons referred to in the course of the poem, are excluded unless they provide useful analogies (e.g. Milton, Wordsworth, Cervantes). Themes and critical points are not indexed.